Contents

Acknowledgments

This book is written through the life experience of many believers and many hands have done the writing. First of all, Catholic people in small church communities (SCC) throughout the world have contributed the life focus questions and statements for each Sunday's lectionary readings. This book is primarily theirs. It gives voice to the people of the Church in their small church communities. Art Baranowski and Jane Hime made and kept contact with small church communities around the globe to compose the sharing questions.

A special thanks is due to Rev. John Castelot, whose syndicated newspaper columns on the Sunday readings provided a resource for the commentaries. The commentaries themselves were written by parishioners of St. Elizabeth Ann Seton Parish and St. Hugh Parish in the Archdiocese of Detroit. Carrie Piro and Sister Trinita Schilling, I.H.M., directed the writing.

Two editing teams, one led by Jane Hime and the other by Carrie and Joe Piro, finalized the faith-sharing statements. Joe Piro prepared the manuscript.

This good work is due to all these fine people, mostly unknown to each other but bonded in the Body of Christ.

Preface

Seventy-five hundred people wrote this book! The life focus statements based on the Sunday readings of the lectionary came from small church communities in Catholic parishes from North America, South America, Asia, Europe, Australia and Africa.

Most of the statements originally came from workshops of the National Alliance for Parishes Restructuring Into Communities (NAPRC) for parishes planning to restructure into small church communities. These ninety workshops took place throughout the United States, Canada and Australia from 1989 through 1993. The parishes represent city, inner-city, suburban and rural areas. English, Spanish, French, Italian, Vietnamese, Filipino, Korean, Hmong and other languages are used in these parishes. Some have ten to fifteen ethnic groups in one parish.

In addition to parishes at the NAPRC workshops, individual small church communities were asked to submit life focus questions for those Sundays not covered. Some Sundays and feasts, for example Pentecost, Christmas, Epiphany and the Triduum, have more than one set of questions.

These small communities share the conviction that the Catholic parish needs to be restructured into small ongoing church communities. In these communities people can help each other connect everyday life with the Scriptures and Tradition of the Church. The pastoral leaders of these small church communities connect them to the wider Church of the parish and diocese (see *Creating Small Faith Communities: A Plan for Restructuring the Parish and Renewing Catholic Life* by Art Baranowski, St. Anthony Messenger Press).

Appendix A includes a description of each small group that submitted life focus questions. Groups in the United States are listed alphabetically according to their archdiocese or diocese. Groups from outside the United States are listed alphabetically by continent and country in Appendix B.

We hope this book will help connect small church communities and parishes involved in restructuring. The royalties will be used to further the work of NAPRC (P.O. Box 1152, Troy, MI 48099). This organization supports parishes that are deliberately and methodically restructuring into small church communities. Since NAPRC is focused on structural change, its work is primarily with parish leaders: priests, staffs, key lay leaders. NAPRC believes that the parish is the most effective unit of the Catholic Church and that the parish will not be healthy or survive well without bringing its people together in a new way.

NAPRC Board Members:

Rev. Arthur Baranowski, Sterling Heights, Michigan, president
Carrie Piro, Novi, Michigan, coordinator
Katie O'Reily, Shelby Township, Michigan, assistant coordinator
Rev. Robert Beloin, North Haven, Connecticut
Rev. Jarlath Cunnane, Altadena, California
Rev. Clem Davis, Indianapolis, Indiana
Msgr. Neal Dolan, Lakeside, California
Rev. James Dunning, Arlington, Virginia
Br. Robert Moriarty, S.M., Bloomfield, Connecticut
Rev. Michael Schneller, New Orleans, Louisiana
Msgr. Thomas Spadaro, Holbrook, New York

Introduction

The life focus questions in this book can be used for homilies, teaching, the Christian Initiation process and pastoral council meetings. The primary use, however, will be to facilitate the life of small church communities. We believe that the parish needs to restructure into ongoing small groups that gradually develop into small church communities. The parish as it is now structured is not reaching the everyday lives and decisions of its people. We also believe that every parishioner can fit into a small community and can make an invaluable personal contribution to the Church by being a member of an SCC.

The experience-sharing format in this book is intended to be used after people in a small community have built up trust in one another and grown a bit into a reflective life-style. This is the third stage in the growth of a small community (see *Creating Small Faith Communities*). At this third stage, the small church community usually meets about twice a month. It has a pastoral facilitator who connects the SCC to the pastoral leaders of the parish.

Format of the SCC

Below is an outline of the format of a regular meeting of a SCC. It consists of the following elements:

Gathering

Review of life

Quiet time with the readings, commentary and questions

Faith sharing
—Small groups (three or four people)
—Large group ("So what?"—life challenge)

Prayer

Break

Study

Gathering

A few minutes are spent settling down and centering on the purpose of the meeting. Helpful examples are:

"How was your day?" (2-3 sentences)

"One thing I enjoyed or was frustrated by today...."

"One concern I brought to this meeting...."

"One experience I look forward to...."

Quiet listening to a piece of music

Singing one or several hymns

Review of Life (in pairs)

Many small communities find this helpful but not necessary. The review of life can be an effective way to be accountable to another person in the Church for a faith life. Staying with the same person for a good length of time makes the review easier and more effective. This helps people be more consistent in the issues they raise. The questions in the review are basic and simple:

Am I making time for reflection and prayer regularly?

What gets in the way?

How is my prayer affecting my family life? workplace? parish? my views on and participation in society? connection with the poor of the world?

What is my one clear resolution?

Faith Sharing (small groups)

Smaller groups of three people do what the larger group cannot. The level of communication is deeper. People say more. Quiet types speak more and a dominant person is more controlled. Spouses usually are not in the same threesome. After a generous period of silence, each person responds from personal experience to whichever Scripture focus statement he or she chooses. Good listening skills have been practiced and learned from previous programs. No advice is given, unless asked; this is not a time for solving problems. Each person takes a turn, with some quiet time between people.

Faith Sharing (large groups)

The SCC consists of eight to twelve people, to maximize communication. This larger group continues the sharing in view of the way the small group experience has deepened each person's insights and experience. A particular person's response in the threesome is never divulged by another to this larger group. The larger group focuses on the question "So what?" This refers to making a connection to one's life after the SCC meeting. What difference will this make in my attitudes or actions in my family, place of work, political involvement or society? The SCC may or may not take on a group service project, but each member makes everyday life efforts toward building God's kingdom.

Prayer (together)

Because prayer is listening as well as talking, all of the listening to life experiences focused through Scripture and Tradition is part of the prayer. The SCC also takes time as a community to listen and respond to the faith sharing that takes place. Being in God's presence together through prayer deepens the bond between the members more than anything else. Prayer is central, not a short closing to the meeting or an afterthought.

The small church community can experience different ways to pray and help people feel comfortable with quiet time. Prayer of petition is only one kind of prayer in the Catholic heritage. Other forms of prayer include praying with Scripture, centering prayer, praying with the imagination, *examen* of consciousness and *lectio divina* (see *Praying Alone and Together* by Rev. Arthur Baranowski, St. Anthony Messenger Press).

Prayer With Symbols and Rituals

Symbols and rituals in life can express what words cannot. When someone we love has experienced a tragedy, taking hold of that person's hand can communicate more than words. The sacraments and rituals of the Church express what cannot be said completely in words only—what God's love means, who we are before God, our bond with each other as we live in God's presence. The Church expresses itself through rituals developed and treasured over two thousand years. One of the ways the SCC stays in touch with the larger Church is through connecting with its rituals.

Below are examples of praying with symbols and rituals that connect with the rituals of the larger Church. Whoever leads the prayer time can adapt these for individual small church communities.

Bible: Large and solid, displayed in a place of honor with cloth, flowers or candle. Can be reverently touched, passed from one person to another, kissed, etc.

Crucifix or cross: Same as above.

Statue, icon, picture of a deceased member: Same as above.

Fire: Always a sign of God's presence, purifying, showing things the way they really are. Can be lit, shared by each lighting a candle from another's or from the Christ Candle, especially when making or renewing a commitment—Easter-Pentecost season, Christmas season, Baptism, Confirmation, Marriage, etc.

Easter Candle, Christ Candle: Same as above.

Water: Death leading to resurrection. Can be displayed in beautiful large clear bowl or shared from one to another, used for the Sign of the Cross or sprinkled. Easter-Pentecost season, Baptism of the Lord, renewal of Baptism or any commitment as a disciple.

Oil: Traditional sign of the power of God's own Spirit to heal, empower for mission, consecrate one's work. Oil is especially symbolic during the Easter-Pentecost season, for anointing in a time of illness, renewal of Baptism or Confirmation, dedication of one's gift or piece of work.

Air or wind: The sign of God's Spirit. Listening to one's own breath, listening to or feeling the wind, seeing its effect.

Bread and wine: A connection to the parish Eucharist. Breaking one loaf and sharing it with one another, sharing one cup. Making a loaf of bread.

Producing these elements. Sharing a simple meal together in which each provides something.

Laying on of hands: The touch of affirmation for healing or being chosen for a particular service.

Signs of hope, waiting: A cloth moving from purple to pink to white (like the gradual sunrise), a growing plant or bulb, a pregnant person or couple, a child. These signs are especially appropriate at Advent and may also be used at other times.

Signs of call, struggle, conversion, journey, search, dying and rising: Sand representing the desert, a cross, a spike, thorn bushes, a growing plant, a dying seed, a barren tree or plant, thorns, darkness, ashes. These can be used during Lent or a particular time of life.

Signs of life after struggle: Lily, willow, eggs, good food. The Easter-Pentecost season celebrates new life.

Signs of surprise at God's going beyond the expected: Light breaking into darkness, incense, gifts, bringing in someone different than ourselves.

Break

Social time in the SCC format is an important part of the experience. Lingering together after the formal meeting offers an opportunity to continue the bonding that has been experienced. Some people may say more significant things during the social time than in any other part of the meeting. Ending with social time allows the meeting to end at the agreed time. People can stay as long as they wish but also feel free to leave. Refreshments usually are simple, making it easy for the next host and not distracting from the main reason for the meeting.

Study

There is room for study, as long as the sharing of life and faith is central to the meeting. For example, an SCC should study how it connects to the larger Church. Also, if some kind of critique of society or culture is to happen eventually, there needs to be some study of how structures and systems in our world keep people poor.

Commentaries and Questions for Cycle A

First Sunday of Advent (A)

Reading I: Isaiah 2:1-5
Reading II: Romans 13:11-14
Gospel: Matthew 24:37-44

Scripture Focus

During Advent we celebrate the coming of Christ not only two thousand years ago, but also at the end of time. Today's readings emphasize that end time. The Gospel reading is part of Matthew's great discourse on the establishment of the Reign of God at the end of time. Jesus tells his followers that they must live their lives in such a way that they are ready to enter into this reign at any time.

Life Focus

1. Relate an experience that made you stop and reflect on your priorities and on the way you live your life.

2. What are some of the difficulties in staying alert to God in your everyday life?

3. If tomorrow were to be the last day of your life, what might you change?

4. Recall a disruptive experience in your life in the past few weeks. How did it affect you?

5. Share a time when you were caught unprepared. How do you see God being a part of that experience?

—Diocese of Phoenix
   Phoenix, Arizona

Second Sunday of Advent (A)

Reading I: Isaiah 11:1-10
Reading II: Romans 15:4-9
Gospel: Matthew 3:1-12

Scripture Focus

In the first reading Isaiah presents a picture of an ideal king and an ideal kingdom. The people's lives would send a message to the world *that God's kingdom is here to stay.* John tells his followers that the time has come for them to reform their lives. His baptism was a ceremony for followers to express their intention of conversion. And John promises that the one to follow him would baptize with the Holy Spirit and with fire, a baptism that would carry the power of God. John confronts the religious leaders of his day and attacks their insincerity. Their religion is only on the outside for people to see. He says that their lives don't show evidence of conversion.

Life Focus

1. Think of those times when your life was a desert place. During those times what did you hear? How did you respond?

2. In what way do you want to reform your life? What does it mean to reform? How will you know that reform is taking place?

3. We all know people who seem to lead fruitful lives. Who are these people in your life? In what ways have their lives affected you?

4. What in your life needs to be improved to prepare for Christ's coming?

—Diocese of Kansas City-St. Joseph
   St. Charles Borromeo Parish
   Kansas City, Missouri

(continued)

1. How does it feel to have your way of life questioned?

2. If you were baptized as an infant, what difference does it make in your life today?

—Diocese of Kansas City
  Guardian Angels Parish
  (Center for Pastoral Life Ministry)
  Kansas City, Missouri

Third Sunday of Advent (A)

Reading I: Isaiah 35:1-6, 10
Reading II: James 5:7-10
Gospel: Matthew 11:2-11

Scripture Focus

Prophets such as Isaiah brought a message of hope that things could be different. John the Baptist, too, proclaimed the coming of a new age. But now, John is in prison and his followers wonder if Jesus is the promised one. They may have been expecting a "fire and brimstone" preacher who would lead the people out of their oppression. Instead, Jesus gives them a different image, an image of healing, forgiveness and tender concern for all people.

Life Focus

1. Describe a false or faulty image you once had of how your life, the world or the Church was supposed to be. What changed your image?

2. Relate an experience when it was easy for you to recognize God in a person, situation or event, and another when it was difficult.

3. What obstacles do you have in your life that keep you from following Christ today? Describe an experience in your life when you removed an obstacle.

4. Describe an experience when you felt hemmed in by your small world. Relate who or what helped to free you from this situation.

—Archdiocese of New Orleans
  Resurrection of Our Lord Church
  New Orleans, Louisiana

Fourth Sunday of Advent (A)

Reading I: Isaiah 7:10-14
Reading II: Romans 1:1-7
Gospel: Matthew 1:18-24

Scripture Focus

Matthew's version of Jesus' conception is a statement of Christian faith in Jesus as the Son of God. It begins with Joseph's confusion over Mary's pregnancy. They were engaged to be married but had not yet lived together. Sexual relations with anyone except the engaged person were considered adultery, and punishment was severe. God reassures Joseph in a dream that the child has been conceived by "the power of the Holy Spirit." Matthew sees Joseph as a model of faith. He recognizes the power of God working in ways he cannot understand. The child's destiny is indicated by his name: The name *Jesus* means "Yahweh helps" or "Yahweh saves." Matthew stresses the meaning of *Emmanuel*, "God-With-Us," to emphasize Jesus' divine Sonship.

Life Focus

1. Describe a time when you felt your trust had been betrayed by someone you loved.

2. Describe a time when you had to struggle to trust God in a difficult situation.

3. When did you change a decision of yours after prayer and reflection?

—Archdiocese of Los Angeles
   Our Lady of the Assumption Church
   Ventura, California

Christmas—Mass at Midnight (ABC)

Reading I: Isaiah 9:1-6
Reading II: Titus 2:11-14
Gospel: Luke 2:1-14

Scripture Focus

Luke records the birth of the child with tender simplicity and stresses the theme of poverty all through his Gospel. The people have reason to be joyful because in David's city a savior is born; he is the Messiah and Lord. These three—Savior, Messiah, Lord—are Luke's favorite titles for Jesus. The song of the angels, "Glory to God in the Highest," is the response. God has sent the Prince of Peace with the fullness of *shalom* (peace and blessings) to all. All are the objects of God's gracious love.

Life Focus

1. Christ came to us as a child. When has a child had an impact on your life?

2. Recall a time God has given a sign to you (a person, a place or an event).

3. Relate a time in your life when you brought "good tidings" to those in need.

—Diocese of Green Bay
   St. Mary of the Angels Parish
   Green Bay, Wisconsin

1. In your life right now, how does the coming of the Messiah bring you peace?

2. What are some things you do to make celebrating Christmas more meaningful than just merry-making?

3. How do you share the joy of Christmas with others?

—Blessed Sacrament Congregation
   Assumption Parish
   Davao City, Philippines

(continued)

1. Describe a time when you were "down and feeling poor" and God blessed you with an unexpected gift.

2. Tell of some ordinary activity or event in your life when you believe God "broke in."

3. When you look around, where is there need for this good news?

—Archdiocese of Cincinnati
   Precious Blood Church
   Dayton, Ohio

Christmas—Mass at Dawn (ABC)

Reading I: Isaiah 62:11-12
Reading II: Titus 3:4-7
Gospel: Luke 2:15-20

Scripture Focus

Some shepherds, a lowly and despised group, were the first to receive the Good News of the birth of a Savior. For the shepherds, to see was to understand. They truly understood what had been told them about this child. When they told the news to others, all were astonished. Mary, reflecting on all these things in her heart, represents all of us who in faith keep searching for understanding.

Life Focus

1. Relate how you felt when you received the news that someone near to you was to give birth.

2. Describe how receiving good—even saving—news affected your life, your community, your family.

3. Because Jesus was born to save the poor in heart, how do you see Jesus saving you in your life today?

4. Jesus was born among us to show us how to live with others. How are we following in his path of love in our life, for example, in receiving visitors and/or neighbors in our village, town, parish?

—All Souls Catholic Mission
   Binga, Zimbabwe

Christmas—Mass During the Day (ABC)

Reading I: Isaiah 52:7-10
Reading II: Hebrews 1:1-6
Gospel: John 1:1-18

Scripture Focus

This Gospel for Christmas Day is the prologue or beginning of John's Gospel. It starts, "In the beginning." This echoes the first line of the Book of Genesis. The connection is clear. The Word (the eternal Son of God) already existed at the instant of creation. He had not been born as a human being and given the name Jesus yet, but he was in the presence of God. It was through God's Word ("Let there be...") that things were created. "Let there be light," the first gift of the creator, was not only the sun, moon and stars, but the light of the Word. Human beings brought evil into God's creation, but that darkness did not overpower the light.

Life Focus

1. Our own Church is a mixture of light and darkness. From your own experience, where has light broken through? From your own own experiences, where are we as a Church still in the dark?

2. Tell of an experience when another person's words revealed God's presence to you.

3. When have your words helped another person see? Where did you find the right words?

4. How have you seen light continue to shine in spite of great darkness all around?

5. If you accept the Word as love, how does this influence those you meet in your daily life?

6. Mary accepted the Word and gave birth to Jesus, the Word made flesh. How do you give birth to Jesus in the world? Give an example.

—Diocese of Wheeling-Charleston
St. Theresa Parish
Morgantown, West Virginia

Feast of the Holy Family (A)

Reading I: Sirach 3:2-6, 12-14
Reading II: Colossians 3:12-21
Gospel: Matthew 2:13-15, 19-23

Scripture Focus

Matthew's story of the "Flight into Egypt" is modeled on the stories of Moses and his escape from the Pharaoh. Matthew's main intent is to say something about who Jesus is. He wants us to make an act of faith in this Jesus. Like the people of Israel escaping from Egypt, Jesus is the new Israel. He is God's son. On a very human level, the Gospel also portrays a "holy" family, in which loving parents go to extreme lengths to protect a threatened child.

Life Focus

1. Relate a time in your life when you experienced family unity in the face of danger, difficulty or crisis. Why was there unity?

2. Relate a time when you experienced family disunity. Why was there disunity?

3. Describe an experience of God guiding you out of danger or difficulty. How did God "speak" to you? Through a friend, family member, a stranger, your feelings, prayer?

4. What can you do to defend and promote gospel values at home, at work, at church and in society? What keeps you from doing it?

—Diocese of Brownsville
St. Paul Church
Mission, Texas

Feast of Epiphany (ABC)

Reading I: Isaiah 60:1-6
Reading II: Ephesians 3:2-3, 5-6
Gospel: Matthew 2:1-12

Scripture Focus

Epiphany means "manifestation," a revelation of Jesus as truly God. Matthew and Luke show this child to be divine through stories of "signs and wonders" when Jesus was an infant. Matthew's account of the visit of the three magi also shows the Church's mission to the Gentiles. Matthew's audience, largely Jewish Christians, was struggling to accept the presence of Gentile Christians in their community. Matthew shows in this Gospel passage that the salvation of Gentiles as well as Jews was indeed God's plan.

Life Focus

1. What helps you stay focused on God's presence in everyday situations where God is usually not mentioned?

2. From your experience, when have you come to appreciate people you used to pass by or not notice?

3. Who and what on your journey has helped you to know and understand Jesus and his message better?

4. How do we reconcile the material gifts we have in our lives with the simple life-style of Jesus?

—Fengshan City
 Taiwan, Republic of China

1. Herod feared losing his power. When have you known people to lie or hurt others because of fear?

2. Who or what event was the star that led you to a better understanding of Jesus?

3. What gifts do you bring to the Christ Child?

4. In your faith journey, when have you taken a different route than you expected?

—Nova Descoberta
 Detroit-Recife Mission
 Brazil

1. The wise men worked hard to find Jesus, and we are asked to do the same. What are some ways you have found Jesus in your life?

2. The wise men were following the star and found Jesus. What can you do to help the Catholic community become a better light in helping others find Jesus?

3. How can you find Christ and worship him?

4. What are the different ways we as a community can be like the star and help other people come and worship Jesus?

—Catechist Training Center Fissoa
 Kavieng, New Ireland Proving
 Papua, New Guinea

(continued)

1. If we are called to make Jesus known to others, how do we deal with the Herods of this world?

2. In my life, who has led or guided me to seek Jesus in a deeper way? How can I be a guide for others?

—Diocese of Kalamazoo
   St. Joseph Church
   Kalamazoo, Michigan

1. Describe an experience in which you felt Jesus' presence during this Christmas season.

2. Relate an experience in which God has been shown to you.

3. Recall an experience of God coming to you in an unexpected way or person.

4. Tell of a time when you anticipated something wonderful was about to happen, but other people were negative.

5. Who helps you see God? Who or what makes believing more difficult?

6. What gifts do I have to offer to God in response to his love?

—Diocese of St. Augustine
   Jacksonville, Florida

Baptism of the Lord (A)

Reading I: Isaiah 42:1-4, 6-7
Reading II: Acts 10:34-38
Gospel: Matthew 3:13-17

Scripture Focus

Our first reading is one of the four "Servant Songs" in the Book of Isaiah. The "servant" is both an individual and someone who stands for all the people. The servant will triumph—but only after suffering. When Jesus comes to be baptized, John is confused. But Jesus reveals the Father to John and declares himself to be the "son" who alone knows God's will. When Jesus comes from the water, the Spirit comes in visible form. Jesus is revealed as "servant," "beloved," "chosen one" with whom God was "well pleased."

Life Focus

1. Give examples from your experience when you expected to be the receiver but turned out to be the giver.

2. Describe a time when you experienced God working through you in a way you had not expected.

3. Identify a way your understanding and appreciation of God evolved throughout your life.

4. Who had been willing to suffer for you? What has been the effect on you?

5. When in your life have you found some peace even in time of turmoil and suffering?

—Diocese of Worcester
   Office of Religious Education
   Worcester, Massachusetts

(continued)

1. Describe an experience when you knew you were loved. Who has helped you believe your life was worthwhile?

2. Relate an incident in your life when you felt God's love.

3. From your personal experience, describe a time you were asked to do something you weren't ready to do.

4. Speak of a time when you found meaning in an event only after you reflected on it.

—Diocese of Nashville
  Catholic Center
  Nashville, Tennessee

First Sunday of Lent (A)

Reading I: Genesis 2:7-9, 3:1-7
Reading II: Romans 5:12, 17-19
Gospel: Matthew 4:1-11

Scripture Focus

Following his baptism, Jesus fasted in the desert for forty days. There he faced the same temptations to stop trusting God's care and power that Adam and Eve faced in the Garden of Eden, the same temptations faced by the Israelites in their forty-year journey through the desert to the Promised Land. Jesus shares the experience of his people but stays faithful and trusting. We now follow Jesus as God's people chosen in the New Covenant. We share his experience and seek the faith he lived so completely.

Life Focus

1. Describe an experience when you felt abandoned but help came.

2. Share an experience in your life when you stayed true to the person you believed in.

3. Relate an experience when you were able to identify God's support in a difficult choice you made.

4. Recall an experience when you had to trust without assurance.

—Archdiocese of Chicago
  Chicago, Illinois

(continued)

1. In what ways has the call to follow Christ brought you into conflict with others?

2. In what ways have you been tempted to abandon the mission to proclaim the Gospel?

3. Have you been able to overcome temptations to water down or give up announcing the Good News in today's world?

—Nirivillo, Chile

1. What was your most recent desert experience?

2. How do you tell true prophets from those who use the Word of God for their own ends?

3. What most easily gets you "off track" from being the person you are called to be? How do you get back "on track"?

4. Jesus' temptations are very clear. How do you identify temptations in your life when they are less obvious?

5. What are the hungers in your life?

—Diocese of Manchester
  Nashua Christian Life Center
  Hudson, New Hampshire

Second Sunday of Lent (A)

Reading I: Genesis 12:1-42
Reading II: 2 Timothy 1:8-10
Gospel: Matthew 17:1-9

Scripture Focus

God calls Abram to leave his own country on the strength of a promise of future greatness. Abram trusts God and goes on trusting through the difficult journeys ahead. In the Gospel Jesus and three of his disciples journey to the top of a mountain, the traditional place where God speaks and shows himself. Jesus again hears his own call, a reminder of who he is and the great trial that lies ahead. Peter, James and John, the same three disciples who will be with him during the agony in the Garden of Gethsemane, are blessed with a vision of Jesus as the risen Lord in all his glory. They hear God's voice and clear call: "This is my beloved Son with whom I am well pleased; listen to him." This vision and call move them down the mountain and toward the promise of glory on the other side of suffering.

Life Focus

1. When in your life were you able to "move on" in spite of fear of the unknown?

2. Describe a time when the joy of the moment gave you a sense that the rest of life was worthwhile.

3. What feelings did you experience when you were required to leave "home" to move to a new place?

—Diocese of Cleveland
  Cleveland, Ohio

(continued)

13

1. Relate a personal or community experience of Jesus calling you to move beyond yourself and your world to heal and liberate others.

2. How have the life and teachings of Jesus helped you to see your own mission in the world?

3. How have you responded to God's message regarding the poor and oppressed?

—Nirivillo, Chile

1. Describe an event in your life when you felt God was calling you to do something. How did you respond? What risks did you face in responding to God's call? How did the risks influence your decision?

2. How have you recognized in your own life God's plan for you?

3. How do you see yourself as a disciple of Jesus? What has it cost you to be a disciple?

4. What risks have you had to take for the sake of the gospel?

5. How have you experienced God's power at work in your life?

6. Have you experienced a change in your life as a result of witnessing God's love to others?

—Diocese of Paterson
  St. Nicholas Roman Catholic Church
  Passaic, New Jersey

1. Relate a time when you followed a faith call from God. Did you answer the call because of faith or for another reason (perhaps you felt it was the right thing to do)?

2. Most of us have a fear of the unknown. Recall a time when you had to deal with the unknown. How did your faith help you and what was the result?

3. Relate an experience when you found it difficult to stand up for what you believe and you compromised your Christian beliefs and went with "the flow."

4. Relate a time when, in spite of difficulty, you stood up for what you believed.

—Archdiocese of Louisville
  St. Bernard Catholic Church
  Louisville, Kentucky

Third Sunday of Lent (A)

Reading I: Exodus 17:3-7
Reading II: Romans 5:1-2, 5-8
Gospel: John 4:5-42

Scripture Focus

Today's Gospel is about the water that gives life, about getting beyond physical thirst to a deeper thirst for trust and love. Jesus draws the Samaritan woman through a solidly physical understanding of thirst and water to an honest look at her life and her need for conversion, and finally a recognition of who he is as the Messiah, the one who will quench all the thirsts of the people. In turn, this woman seeks out the townspeople and invites them to meet Jesus. Conversion is a slow process, but the patient persistence of Jesus will quench our thirst—in spite of ourselves. And it always moves us beyond our own nourishment to an active involvement in the lives of others.

Life Focus

1. Describe an experience when a barrier in your life was broken down.

2. What have you experienced that was so exciting you had to share it?

3. Who are the individuals or groups in your life from whom you are least likely to hear truth?

4. Relate an experience when you've found freedom through another.

5. Where or to whom do you go to be refreshed?

6. When has another drawn "living water" from you?

7. What are your "thirsts"?

—Diocese of Tucson
  Tucson, Arizona

1. What do you learn about the qualities of Jesus in this Gospel? How do you feel about this? Relate the message to your life experience.

2. What can you learn from the openness of the Samaritan woman that is necessary for your growth as a person and a Christian? Relate this message to your life experience.

—Diocese of Reno-Las Vegas
  St. Andrew Church
  Boulder City, Nevada

Fourth Sunday of Lent (A)

Reading I: 1 Samuel 16:1, 6-7, 10-13
Reading II: Ephesians 5:8-14
Gospel: John 9:1-41

Scripture Focus

The themes of light and seeing come up again and again in today's readings. In the first reading Samuel is reminded to see others through God's eyes: "Not as [a human being] sees does God see, because [a human being] sees the appearance, but the Lord looks into the heart." And the whole drama of today's Gospel revolves around those who see and those who fail to see. Sight in this story becomes a symbol of belief. Blindness is about more than just not being able to see with the eyes; it's about the refusal to believe.

Life Focus

1. Speak of a time when simple or broken people saw things more clearly than the people who seem to have it all together.

2. Talk about an experience when healing or insight came in an unexpected way.

3. Relate an experience when you were blind to God's love.

4. Relate an experience when your everyday rules and routines have kept you from "seeing" God.

5. Name a time when someone helped you change a negative attitude.

—Diocese of Providence
  Providence, Rhode Island

1. How did prejudices and fixed ideas against Christianity block or delay your acceptance of Jesus as Lord?

2. At times of self-pity because of your own or a loved one's affliction, how did you come to see "the works of God" displayed?

3. How have you reached out to share your faith and love with people around you?

—St. Augustine Kasai Catholic Church
  Tokyo, Japan

1. Describe an experience in your life when because of a difficult time your faith was affected (for better or worse).

2. Relate an experience when you were afraid to share God's goodness in your life. What were you afraid of?

3. Describe an experience in your life when you placed your trust in someone. What happened?

4. Recall some things you used to believe about life, which you no longer hold to be true.

5. Relate an experience when someone tried to make you conform to another's beliefs.

—Diocese of Allentown
  St. John the Baptist Church
  Whitehall, Pennsylvania

Fifth Sunday of Lent (A)

Reading I: Ezekiel 37:12-14
Reading II: Romans 8:8-11
Gospel: John 11:1-45

Scripture Focus

Today's readings marvel at the creative, life-giving power of God. Ezekiel tells us that the God who can transform lifeless bones into vital human beings can restore a nation from the death of exile to a life of freedom. Paul tells the Romans that the power of the Spirit brings our mortal bodies to life through the creative, transforming presence of the Spirit of God dwelling in us. In the Gospel we see a marvelously dramatic example of the power of God to bring life out of death. The essential message for us is Jesus' pronouncement: "I am the resurrection and the life; whoever believes in me, even if he dies, will live, and everyone who lives and believes in me will never die" (John 11:25).

Life Focus

1. Relate a time when you made a decision because of friendship. What were the consequences? Did it mean going along with the crowd or with Christ?

2. Describe an instance when you denied yourself some extravagant want. How did the denial increase your faith?

3. Imagine some of the emotions and feelings that Lazarus might have experienced on "the first day of the rest of his life." Describe a time when you experienced some of these feelings in your life. Did it change you?

4. Have you been able to allow God to open any of the graves you dug yourself and heal you?

5. As your days pass by, what are the small "resurrections" that keep you conscious of God in your life?

—Diocese of Tulsa
  St. James Parish
  Bartlesville, Oklahoma

1. What keeps you from stepping out of your "living tomb"?

2. Relate an experience that kept you entombed and from which you were able to come forth.

3. Describe a time when you were able to "untie" someone and set the person free.

4. During these last days of Lent, what do you need to change in order to rise to the new life which Jesus offers you?

—Archdiocese of Baltimore
  St. Isaac Jogues Church
  Baltimore, Maryland

Passion/Palm Sunday (A)

Reading I: Isaiah 50:4-7
Reading II: Philippians 2:6-11
Gospel: Matthew 26:14-27, 66

Scripture Focus

The crowds demand that Jesus "be crucified." In this, they side with the religious leaders. Two of Jesus' chosen disciples also side with values opposed to those Jesus taught and lived. Judas betrays the Lord to the authorities; Peter, who was first among the apostles and first to confess Jesus as the Son of the Living God, now denies that same Jesus out of fear for his own life. Jesus, the obedient Son, deliberately chooses to be faithful to God's values even though it led to his death. He dies, as he lived, carrying out God's will.

Life Focus

1. Describe a time in your life when a job, task or money became more important than someone you loved.

2. Speak of a person you know who stood alone to stay true to the values of his or her life. How did it influence you?

3. Share a time when you were faithful to God's call despite personal sacrifices.

—Diocese of Green Bay
  St. Mary of the Angels Church
  Black Creek, Wisconsin

1. Relate a time when you or others suffered because of racial discrimination.

2. Name a time in your life when Christ's death and resurrection had a special meaning to you.

3. When have you experienced the joy of the Eucharist at times other than the celebration of the Mass?

—Sao Paulo
  Puno, Peru

Holy Thursday (ABC)

Reading I: Exodus 12:1-8, 11-14
Reading II: 1 Corinthians 11:23-26
Gospel: John 13:1-15

Scripture Focus

When the Jewish people remembered an event, the past became present for them once again. The Jews remembered the first Passover, when God led them from slavery, with a yearly Passover Meal. In celebrating that meal, they renewed their commitment to the covenant. Jesus celebrates this Passover Meal as a Jewish "father" with his family of disciples. Today when we remember him in this meal, Jesus is present with us. Jesus shows his disciples and us what being his people in the new covenant means. He stoops to wash the apostles' feet, and he tells them to do the same for each other. This night we remember and celebrate who we are—our service to each other and the world, the role of our priests and the gift of the Eucharist.

Life Focus

1. What have you done to follow Jesus' example of washing the feet of each other?

2. In what practical way have you allowed another to wash your feet?

3. What barriers do you have to remove in order to love and serve others?

—Hope Community
  Wolverhampton, England

(continued)

1. What in you hinders you from "washing the feet" of your brothers and sisters in distress?

2. Relate a time in your life when, like Peter, you refused the kindness of others.

3. Relate a time when your Catholic Christian faith was more centered on self-and-God. Relate a time when it centered on serving others as Jesus does in the Gospel.

—St. Augustine Kasai Catholic Church
  Tokyo, Japan

1. Share a time when a peer, authority figure, member of the opposite sex or a poor person offered to help you, and your response was similar to Simon Peter's. What made you react that way and how did you feel?

2. The Lord invites you to be of service to others. How have you responded?

3. The Lord continues to serve you. How are you experiencing his service in your life today?

—Diocese of Harrisburg
  St. Joseph Parish
  York, Pennsylvania

1. Describe a time when you felt cleansed (physical, mental or spiritual cleansing).

2. Relate a situation when you chose to do a menial or unpleasant task for someone simply out of love. How did this bring you closer to God's love?

3. Describe how someone else followed Jesus' example and "washed your feet."

4. What have you done this past week that you would like others to remember after your death?

—Diocese of Fort Wayne-South Bend
  St. Monica Parish
  Mishawaka, Indiana

Good Friday (ABC)

Reading I: Isaiah 52:13—53:12
Reading II: Hebrews 4:14-16, 5:7-9
Gospel: John 18:1—19:42

Scripture Focus

Good Friday only makes sense if it is joined to Easter Sunday. For Jesus, this is "his hour"—the time of his passage home to his Father. In John's account of the Passion, Jesus is the king, and his kingship shines through all his humiliation and suffering. He lays his life down willingly. John mentions that the lambs are being slaughtered for the Passover. Jesus, the lamb of God who takes away the sins of the world, becomes the lamb on the cross. Jesus is the suffering servant who stands with sinners and takes their life upon himself. He did this willingly, and God will make sure this suffering servant becomes a conquerer and gives new life to all people, Jews and Gentiles alike.

Life Focus

1. How do you feel when you read that Jesus, our Savior, is to be captured and killed?

2. The death of Jesus our Savior shows us that we are to grow in faith and communal life. How do you show that you believe this?

3. Given that we have been saved in Christ who suffered and died for us, do you fear suffering and death? Why?

4. Following Jesus Christ's example to save others, relate some ways you are an evangelizer to those who thirst for Christ.

5. How have you seen in your life that the experience of death can be overcome by faith?

6. How are you experiencing the suffering of Jesus in your life today?

—All Souls Catholic Mission
  Binga, Zimbabwe

(continued)

19

1. Jesus allowed himself to be arrested and chose to go this way to his death on the cross. When have you chosen the path of suffering in order to uphold Christian values?

2. Jesus didn't defend himself when questioned by Pilate. Tell of a time when you did not defend yourself when attacked for doing what was right.

3. Relate a time when you were encouraged to face a difficult and painful situation because of Jesus' passion.

—Broken Wall Community
  Cape Town, South Africa

1. Relate an experience of physical, spiritual or mental suffering in your life that resulted in something good for you.

2. What experience have you had of a friend turning his or her back on you?

3. Relate a time when it was difficult to admit to someone that you were a follower of Jesus.

4. Share a time when you have asked Jesus to help shoulder your burden. How do you want Jesus to help you today?

—Archdiocese of New York
  Church of St. Francis Xavier
  New York, New York

1. Have you ever refused to go that extra mile to aid a friend because of rules, peer pressure or embarrassment? How did you handle the situation?

2. When have you witnessed a person wrongfully accused and you came to this person's defense? If your actions made things more difficult for you, did that influence you?

3. Has someone you love betrayed you? How did you react to this betrayal? Were you able to forgive? If not, what stops you from forgiving?

4. Because of fear, Pilate does not do what he knows is right. Has fear ever kept you from taking a stand against injustice? Has fear ever kept you from speaking out on civil rights, abortion, war, capital punishment, equality, prejudice? Explain.

—Archdiocese of St. Louis
  Sts. John and James Church
  Ferguson, Missouri

Easter Vigil (ABC)

Gospel: Matthew 28:1-10 (A)
Gospel: Mark 16:1-8 (B)
Gospel: Luke 24:1-12 (C)

Scripture Focus

Matthew, Mark and Luke all include Resurrection accounts in their Gospels. In spite of differences in details, the message is the same—Jesus is risen. The three accounts share certain basic elements. The women find an empty tomb, which by itself is a sign only if a person has faith. In Matthew and Mark, the women are told that Jesus will go ahead of his brothers and sisters and meet them in Galilee. In Luke, the disciples are reminded that Jesus spoke of all this before he died. They are told, Don't look for the living one among the dead.

Life Focus

1. The women were the first to the tomb and brought the message to the disciples. What women in your life have conveyed strength and insight?

2. When has Jesus' resurrection touched you in a time of grief, despair or fear?

3. What in you needs to die before you can be revitalized?

4. What has had to die in this small church community so God could bring you to a new life?

—Post Green Community
Dorset, England

1. Describe an incident that evoked fear in the beginning but gave you strength in the end.

2. In what way have you found new courage and hope in the midst of fear and confusion?

3. When did you expect failure but were shocked by success?

4. Name a time when your life began in a new and unexpected way.

—Archdiocese of New Orleans
New Orleans, Louisiana

1. Describe a "coming back to life" experience in your personal life or in your small church community.

2. Women play an important role at the foot of the cross and at the empty tomb. What women played an important role in your faith life? How?

3. How does the Resurrection story call us to share the Good News of Jesus with others? Name a specific way you will do this in the coming week.

—St. Jude Thaddeus Small Christian Community
Musoma, Tanzania

Easter Sunday (ABC)

Reading I: Acts 10:34, 37-43
Reading II: Colossians 3:1-4
Gospel: John 20:1-9

Scripture Focus

All the Gospels agree that women were the first to come to the tomb. Mary Magdalene is always mentioned among them. The scene symbolizes a new creation brought about by the Resurrection of the Light of the world. The darkness suggests the darkness that covered the abyss before light first appeared. When Mary Magdalene sees the stone removed from the entrance, she runs to the disciples with the news that "the Lord has been taken from the tomb!" She saw him die a few days ago, and that prevents her from drawing any other conclusion. The two disciples run side by side to the tomb. Peter sees the burial cloth and the cloth that covered Jesus' head, but he doesn't know how to interpret what he sees. The other disciple, the one Jesus loved and the source of this account, is the first to understand the significance of the empty tomb: "The Lord has risen." For John, all those who came to believe would be loved by Jesus and would love in return.

Life Focus

1. When has the funeral or wake of a friend or relative had an impact on your life?

2. When have you blamed someone and found you had wrongly accused that person? What did you do then?

3. When were your first impressions of a person or a situation proved to be wrong?

4. Have you seen a sign, a hint of the Resurrection in your life? In your family? Your community? The world?

5. Relate a time when you had a stone (barrier) in your faith life removed.

—Nova Descoberta
 Detroit-Recife Mission
 Brazil

1. What are your feelings about a woman being the bearer of the gospel message?

2. Recount an experience in your life that left you feeling like an "empty tomb," as if the Lord had been taken away from you. How did you try to find the Lord again later?

3. Describe a time when you had to deliver a message or request to Church leaders, clergy or laity. How did they listen to what you said?

4. The other disciple (the one Jesus loved) enters the tomb. What he saw there made such an impression on him that he believed at once. Describe a similar experience in your own life when you felt strong convictions despite the lack of external evidence.

—Diocese of El Obeid
 El Obeid, Sudan

1. Name a time in your life when something good came out of a seemingly hopeless situation.

2. Relate an experience from your life when inner peace came from facing a painful situation.

3. Who are you more like: Mary Magdalene, Peter or the Beloved Disciple? Why?

—Diocese of Rockford
 Sts. Peter and Paul Church
 Cary, Illinois

1. Tell of a time in your life when understanding a life situation was difficult.

2. What experience has occurred in your life to cement your faith in someone?

—Diocese of San Jose
 St. Maria Goretti Parish
 San Jose, California

(continued)

22

1. Recall an experience when you took the role of the "beloved disciple."

2. What in your life keeps people from seeing Jesus in you?

3. Recall an experience in your life when your trust in Jesus was shaken. How did you recover?

4. In what ways do you need to become more alive in your faith?

—Archdiocese of Detroit
　St. Elizabeth Ann Seton Parish
　Troy, Michigan

Second Sunday of Easter (A)

Reading I: Acts 2:42-47
Reading II: 1 Peter 1:3-9
Gospel: John 20:19-31

Scripture Focus

Today's readings center on faith. Acts tells us the early community of believers took the gospel to heart and formed their lives on its message. Peter writes to encourage the newly baptized Christians who faced hostility. And the Gospel tells the story of Thomas. He insists upon physical evidence before he believes. He doubts, but Jesus knows this and speaks to him through his doubts. He recognizes Thomas as one who can believe and he calls him to faith. The gospel writer encourages his audience to believe in Jesus even though they haven't actually seen him.

Life Focus

1. When did you believe because of a sign and not by faith?

2. Name a time when you believed by faith.

3. Share an experience when you hesitated to admit that you were a Catholic.

4. Relate a time when you overcame your doubts and became stronger in your relationship with God.

5. When have you ever felt "sent" by the Lord?

6. Relate a time when you did something to help strengthen someone's belief.

7. What hinders you from believing in Jesus in your life?

8. Do you ever identify with Thomas in your spiritual life, and how do you handle periods of doubt?

—Archdiocese of Detroit
　St. Elizabeth Ann Seton Parish
　Troy, Michigan

Third Sunday of Easter (A)

Reading I: Acts 2:14, 22-28
Reading II: 1 Peter 1:17-21
Gospel: Luke 24:13-35

Scripture Focus

Today's Gospel teaches that God's Messiah *had to suffer* before entering into the glory of his risen life. The failure to grasp both aspects, suffering and glory, led many to reject Jesus. The two disciples on the road to Emmaus represent those whose hopes were dashed. If they had understood all the prophecies, not merely those promising a glorious Messiah, they would have realized that Jesus' sufferings were necessary to God's plan. The disciples invite their companion to have supper with them, and in the breaking of the bread, a familiar gesture of Jesus, they finally recognize their Lord. He will likewise be present to future generations in broken bread. Because there is no need to see him physically, "he vanished from their sight."

Life Focus

1. When have your eyes been opened so that you recognized the Lord walking with you?

2. Relate a time when you had to suffer before you experienced the presence of the Lord.

3. What do you need right now to help you continue in your journey of faith?

—Archdiocese of Detroit
   St. Elizabeth Ann Seton Parish
   Troy, Michigan

1. Relate an experience that helped you recognize Jesus in your life.

2. What keeps you from recognizing Jesus in all the events of your daily life?

3. How has a special companion in your journey helped you to know Jesus better?

4. Relate an experience when you invited someone into your conversation, activities or sharing at your table. What was the result and how did you feel?

—Diocese of Honolulu
   Sacred Heart Church
   Honolulu, Hawaii

1. What has been a disappointment in your life that turned out to be a blessing?

2. When one of your own dreams was shattered and all you could talk about was the loss, what helped you to see new possibilities?

3. Can you remember a time when you set your heart on something and were deeply disappointed? What helped you to make it through that difficult time?

4. Have you ever felt like a failure, or like you really made the wrong choice for your life? What helped you to open your eyes to new possibilities for your life?

5. Can you remember a time when everything happening around you told you that what you believed in (set your heart/hopes on) was false? Were you able to keep on believing? What helped you?

6. What meal or gathering have you been part of that has meant something very special to you? Why?

7. Name a road in your life that was different than you expected and discuss what helped you walk that road.

8. Name a person who has helped you while you were on a difficult road in life and talk about what that person did or said that helped you.

—Diocese of Nashville
   Catholic Center
   Nashville, Tennessee

Fourth Sunday of Easter (A)

Reading I: Acts 2:14, 36-41
Reading II: 1 Peter 2:20-25
Gospel: John 10:1-10

Scripture Focus

The image of God as Israel's shepherd was used over and over again in the Hebrew Scriptures. Jesus in John's Gospel uses this image when he describes himself as the Good Shepherd. When sheep were away from the sheepfold, they spent the night within a walled enclosure. The shepherd would lie down in the opening, thus becoming a gate to the enclosure. Moreover, sheep respond only to the voice of their own shepherd. Jesus explains more fully: He is the gate; he alone is the means of access to God. He is the good shepherd who calls followers to himself and leads them to God. He brings his flock not only security but life to the full, even now, in the life of the eternal God.

Life Focus

1. When did you give guidance to someone that would lead them to follow the way of Christ?

2. What are your qualities, strengths and weaknesses that help you or others to follow the Good Shepherd?

—Archdiocese of Anchorage
   Friends of Jesus Prayer Group
   Anchorage, Alaska

1. In what ways have you responded to God's call during this last week (or month)?

2. Relate an experience when you heard God's call and followed that call.

3. Share your experience of God protecting you from false people. How did you hear the Master's voice?

4. As we work toward creating small communities, how do you see the revelation of Jesus working in these communities?

—Diocese of Rockhampton
   Callide Valley Parish
   Biloela Q, Australia

Fifth Sunday of Easter (A)

Reading I: Acts 6:1-7
Reading II: 1 Peter 2:4-9
Gospel: John 14:1-12

Scripture Focus

Today's Gospel is taken from Jesus' long speech at the Last Supper. When he announces his departure, the disciples are understandably sad, but he consoles them with warm words of hope: Through his death they will go to the Father. The central verse of this Gospel, when Jesus identifies himself as "the way, the truth, and the life," reveals Jesus not only as the "way" *to* the Father, but as the revelation *of* the Father. In his *humanity*, he reveals what God is like. Jesus' kindness, his compassion, his concern for the poor, his forgiveness of sinners help us to know the Father.

Life Focus

1. Relate an experience when you did something for others because they valued and trusted you.

2. Describe an experience when you had to trust without knowing what would happen.

3. Tell of an experience that showed a wavering of faith on your part.

4. Describe a personal experience when you wanted someone to show you the way.

5. Where is home for you?

6. Where do you feel like a stranger? Why?

—Archdiocese of Los Angeles
  Los Angeles, California

Sixth Sunday of Easter (A)

Reading I: Acts 8:5-8, 14-17
Reading II: 1 Peter 3:15-18
Gospel: John 14:15-21

Scripture Focus

In today's Gospel Jesus assures his disciples that he will not leave them abandoned, defenseless orphans. He will continue to be with them but in a new way, namely, through the presence of the Holy Spirit. The faithful, those with eyes enlightened by faith, will be deeply aware that he is there with them. He will be not only "with" them, but "within" them, a source of inner strength and confidence. Christians are caught up into the very life of God! For us, this means the Spirit will enable us to find Christ in ourselves and each other.

Life Focus

1. Describe a time when you felt left out, orphaned or abandoned.

2. Relate an example in which an act of loving service brought about healing, excitement or rejoicing.

3. Describe a situation in which you knew that God was present.

4. What signs helped you to recognize God's presence?

—Archdiocese of Cincinnati
  Middletown/Franklin, Ohio

Seventh Sunday of Easter (A)

Reading I: Acts 1:12-14
Reading II: 1 Peter 4:13-16
Gospel: John 17:1-11

Scripture Focus

In Luke's view the glorification of Jesus ushered in a new era. Just as God formed a covenant community with the Jewish people at Sinai, so now he is about to form a new people on the anniversary of that event—Pentecost. Just as Luke told us that Jesus was "at prayer" when the Spirit descended upon him at his Baptism to give him power for his mission, so now the community is at prayer as they await the coming of the Holy Spirit. In the Gospel Jesus entrusts to his followers the message God entrusted to him. Because it will not be easy to carry this message to a hostile world, Jesus prays in a special way for his disciples. He will live on in them, present to the world in a unique and special way.

Life Focus

1. Think of two ways that help you get to know Jesus better. Who, what, when, where?

2. How do you pray best? What do you need?

—Archdiocese of Detroit
St. Elizabeth Ann Seton Parish
Troy, Michigan

1. Recall your earliest introductions to prayer. Who was the focal point of the prayer? How do your prayers differ today?

2. Carrying the message to a hostile world will not be easy for the disciples. When were you happy that you completed some work that you really dreaded to start?

3. Jesus is the Lord of my life. What difference does this make in the way I will live my life this month?

—Archdiocese of Omaha
Omaha, Nebraska

Pentecost Sunday (ABC)

Reading I: Acts 2:1-11
Reading II: 1 Corinthians 12:3-7, 12-13
Gospel: John 20:19-23

Scripture Focus

Our readings today give us two accounts of the Pentecost event. In Luke's account "a driving wind" is heard. In John's, the Lord "breathes" upon his disciples. The apostles, even though they have been gathered together in the upper room out of fear, are now given the power of the Holy Spirit, the life-giving heart of the Church. They are also to do what Jesus did: forgive sins, heal divisions, bring about reconciliation and joy to all. All Christians are commissioned and given power to carry on this mission.

Life Focus

1. Describe how some person has inspired courage in you.

2. What gifts of the Spirit can you identify in yourself that could help transform your world?

3. Which gifts of the Spirit can you identify in our community?

4. How are we developing together with other laypersons a mission of liberation in our everyday life?

—Sao Paulo
Puno, Peru

(continued)

27

1. Describe a time of fear or suffering when you got together with friends for consolation. How did you all find strength to face your problems?

2. Recount a time in your life when, paralleling the situation of the apostles, you were "afraid, behind closed doors." What helped you to "unlock the doors" and overcome your fear?

3. Language is important in sharing the Christian message with others. Recall an experience when your words were terribly misunderstood.

4. How have you recently been able to share peace with someone who was not at peace? When you need peace, where do you seek it?

—Diocese of El Obeid
  El Obeid, Sudan

1. At Pentecost the Spirit enabled the disciples to overcome their fears. What fears were you able to overcome so you could continue the work you were called to do?

2. When have you been surprised at people very different from you hearing God's message through you?

3. Speak of a time when you needed help to forgive someone. What do you find most difficult to forgive in yourself?

—Catholic Parish
  Fengshan City
  Taiwan, Republic of China

1. Relate a time when you wanted to (or did) shut yourself off from life around you. Who brought you out again?

2. What do the words "I'm sending you" call you to do this week?

3. Think about a time when you felt bound by someone's unforgiveness or your own. Describe how you felt when you were forgiven or when you could forgive.

—Diocese of Port Pirie
  Whyalla West Parish-Our Lady Help of Christians Church
  Whyalla Stuart, Australia

1. What causes you to lock your "inner door"? What helps you at those times?

2. Speak of a time when you were able to go beyond your limitations in speaking or doing something.

—Diocese of Spokane
  St. Mary Parish
  Spokane, Washington

The Body and Blood of Christ (A)

Reading I: Deuteronomy 8:2-3, 14-16
Reading II: 1 Corinthians 10:16-17
Gospel: John 6:51-58

Scripture Focus

Jesus provides "real food" and "real drink" in the Eucharist—his own "flesh" and "blood" to sustain the believer. In today's Gospel the crowds find this hard to believe, but Jesus doesn't retreat from his statement. There is no question of Jesus' meaning: When we partake of the Eucharist, we have a share in eternal life—here and now. For John eternal life is God's life, the life God *shares* with his Son. When we receive the Eucharist, we are united to Jesus and the Father. We *share* God's life. When we share Christ's life, we are already living eternally!

Life Focus

1. Recall a celebration of the Mass that meant a lot to you.

2. People quarreled over Jesus and what he expected of them. What does he expect of you in your life?

3. Christ gave us fullness of life. Describe what fullness of life is for you.

4. Although receiving the body and blood of Christ is personal, it is not private. Christ gave us himself for "the life of the world." What commitments does the Eucharist call you to?

5. The Body of Christ on the altar, the Body of Christ around the altar: How are they the same? How different? How do they affect one another?

—Archdiocese of Philadelphia
 St. William Catholic Church
 Philadelphia, Pennsylvania

Trinity Sunday (A)

Reading I: Exodus 34:4-6, 8-9
Reading II: 2 Corinthians 13:11-13
Gospel: John 3:16-18

Scripture Focus

In today's second reading Paul calls the Corinthians to be a community united in Christ. He reminds them that the God to whom they have committed themselves is a God of *love*, who gave us his only Son. The love and the power that brings the Father and the Son together with each other is the Holy Spirit. The very Spirit of God is what brings us together as well—in the Church, in our families and in our small church community. In the Gospel Jesus declares that he is God's only Son, the one who has come from God. He is the means through whom salvation will be given. And this salvation that God confers is based on faith. Those who believe that Jesus is the Son of God will be saved, while others will condemn themselves by their refusal to believe.

Life Focus

1. How have you experienced the Spirit challenging and nudging you?

2. Who are the saviors in your life? How are they Christ to you?

—Diocese of London
 Essex County
 Cottam, Ontario, Canada

1. What part of the world do you find most difficult to love? Why? What part of your own personal world is hardest for you to love?

2. What does it mean to you that you have the power to condemn yourself? Relate a time when you condemned yourself.

—Diocese of Erie
 St. Mark Catholic Center
 Erie, Pennsylvania

Second Sunday of Ordinary Time (A)

Reading I: Isaiah 49:3, 5-6
Reading II: 2 Corinthians 1:1-3
Gospel: John 1:29-34

Scripture Focus

In Christ, God shows the saving plan for the human race. We understand that plan when we appreciate who Christ Jesus is. The first reading speaks of a Servant of God who will not only restore the survivors of Israel after the Babylonian exile but will also be a light for all peoples and nations. The early Church saw Jesus as this servant who gives his life for all and brings about a new world. John speaks of him as the lamb of God who will take away the sins of the world.

Life Focus

1. Share a time when God was working in your life, but you did not know it until later.

2. When or how have you been slow to recognize God in a particular person?

3. Tell of a person in your life whom you came to recognize as special.

4. Describe a time in your life when God's activity surprised you.

5. Where does your world need to be remade and recreated?

—Diocese of Joliet
  Joliet, Illinois

Third Sunday of Ordinary Time (A)

Reading I: Isaiah 8:23—9:3
Reading II: 2 Corinthians 1:10-13, 17
Gospel: Matthew 4:12-23

Scripture Focus

In today's Gospel Jesus begins his public ministry in Capernaum, a seacoast town in Galilee. There, the light of God's saving action begins to shine. Matthew also tells the story of the call of the first disciples. They seem to answer right away and leave everything behind.

Life Focus

1. What did you let go of in your life in order to bring light and healing into the life of another recently?

2. Describe a time this week when you made an effort to change. Share an experience when you were asked to make a change in your life.

3. Describe your struggle when asked to do something that took you from familiar surroundings or routine.

4. Name an experience—difficult or pleasant—when you noted God drawing your attention.

5. Describe the specific areas or activities in your life that are obstacles to following the Lord.

—Diocese of San Diego
  San Diego, California

(continued)

1. Describe a time when you moved from a sense of gloom and confusion to a sense of peace. How did you get there?

2. Describe an experience in the last two weeks when you were having a bad day and someone else brightened your day.

3. Talk about a time that called for painful self-discipline but from which came unforeseen good.

4. When have you settled for less in your life only to find out what you settled for wasn't enough?

5. Name an experience when you found courage in a dark moment.

—Diocese of Youngstown
  Youngstown, Ohio

Fourth Sunday of Ordinary Time (A)

Reading I: Zephaniah 2:3; 3:12-13
Reading II: 1 Corinthians 18:15-20
Gospel: Matthew 5:1-12

Scripture Focus

The Beatitudes, which we hear in this Gospel passage, are the heart of the Sermon on the Mount. Jesus says that the ones who will be "happy" are those whom society has judged unhappy, even wretched. "The poor in spirit" see through the illusion of wealth and, with nothing else to rely on, come to depend on God. The sorrowing bemoan the sad state of a world that neglects God's wishes. The meek and lowly do not presume to act independently of God. Christians seek happiness by striving to imitate God's readiness to forgive. They are called to be single-hearted in doing God's will rather than making self-interest their primary motivation. They must make peace, doing everything in their power to bring this blessing that God holds out to people.

Life Focus

1. Which of the Beatitudes had the most impact on you as they were read? Why?

2. Who or what experience has helped you to value what money can't buy?

3. What does society say makes people happy? What really makes people happy? What makes you happy?

4. In Matthew, Jesus' recipe for happiness differs from the world's. Share a time when you tried to live according to one of the Beatitudes. How did it affect you?

—Diocese of San Diego
  Our Lady of Perpetual Help
  Lakeside, California

Fifth Sunday of Ordinary Time (A)

Reading I: Isaiah 58:7-10
Reading II: 1 Corinthians 2:1-5
Gospel: Matthew 5:13-16

Scripture Focus

Isaiah reminds the people that if they learn to care for one another, they will be able to receive God's care. Their rituals must express a genuine conversion of their hearts. They cannot fast expecting to twist God's arm. Jesus likewise calls his followers to conduct their lives so that they will call attention to the presence of God within them. Salt, light and a city on a hill are clear ways to show what this message means.

Life Focus

1. Who in your life might help you find courage, meaning, energy for living?

2. When were you able to brighten someone's day?

3. Relate a time when someone said, "I'm happy you were here."

—Diocese of Fort Wayne-South Bend
  South Bend, Indiana

Sixth Sunday of Ordinary Time (A)

Reading I: Sirach 15:15-20
Reading II: 1 Corinthians 2:6-10
Gospel: Matthew 5:17-37

Scripture Focus

Jesus certainly believed that the Law of Moses was connected to the reign of God he came to announce. He tells his followers that he came not to abolish but to fulfill the Law, meaning that his message demanded that people go beyond the letter of the Law to the spirit behind it. Christian life beyond the Law was more, not less, demanding than a strict keeping of each little rule of the Law. Jesus promised that the spirit of the Law would lead the people to the fullness of the reign of God.

Life Focus

1. Remember an experience when keeping "just the letter of the law" was not enough for you.

2. Relate an experience when rules and regulations began as an obstacle but became an opportunity to grow in faith.

3. Name an experience when you broke from what was expected of you.

—Archdiocese of Newark
  Annunciation Parish
  Paramus, New Jersey

Seventh Sunday of Ordinary Time (A)

Reading I: Leviticus 19:1-2, 17-18
Reading II: 1 Corinthians 3:16-23
Gospel: Matthew 5:38-48

Scripture Focus

Today's passage continues the Sermon on the Mount. Jesus asks his followers to live by a higher law than the Mosaic code, replacing strict justice with deep concern for the welfare of others. Christians must rise above an ordinary human standard that says we love those who love us in return. Christianity challenges us to love our enemies. Jesus calls us to follow his example. His life mirrors God's love for all creation. We are to love not because others deserve love but because as Christians—followers of Christ, sons and daughters of God—it's our nature to love.

Life Focus

1. When did you have (or not have) the courage to go the extra mile?

2. Describe an experience when you felt injured by someone and struggled to love that person anyhow.

3. Relate a personal experience when you acted differently than you felt, when you acted out of love.

4. Recall a time when the attitude or activity of another person made you angry. Did the anger control your actions or your attitude? For how long? How did you break free?

5. Describe an experience in which you either prayed for or went out of your way to be kind to someone who had wronged you. What change did you feel in yourself?

6. Relate a time when you tried to "turn the other cheek" and it worked. Relate a time when you tried to "turn the other cheek" and it did not work. Relate a time when *you* were the wrongdoer and another person never quit loving you.

—Diocese of Toledo
Toledo, Ohio

Eighth Sunday of Ordinary Time (A)

Reading I: Isaiah 49:14-15
Reading II: 1 Corinthians 4:1-5
Gospel: Matthew 6:24-34

Scripture Focus

Today's Gospel challenges us to put our trust only in God. Jesus tells his followers, "You cannot give yourself to God and money." The operative words here are "give yourself." To live a responsible life in today's world, we must deal with financial concerns. But when this concern becomes an obsession, money (or a career) becomes one's goal, one's god, one's master. What we are and what we have are gifts from God. Excessive worry indicates a lack of trust in God.

Life Focus

1. Relate a recent experience when you trusted someone else completely.

2. Relate a period in your life when you felt it necessary to get your priorities straight.

3. Relate an experience when you had to be dependent on another.

4. Describe an experience when someone completely trusted in you.

5. Share one way you will appreciate the life you have this coming week.

—Diocese of Harrisburg
York, Pennsylvannia

33

Ninth Sunday of Ordinary Time (A)

Reading I: Deuteronomy 11:18, 26-28
Reading II: Romans 3:21-15, 28
Gospel: Matthew 7:21-27

Scripture Focus

Today's reading is the conclusion of the final teaching from the Sermon on the Mount. We must determine God's will for us and give God glory, seeking no recognition for ourselves. Jesus is both model and teacher in this. Simply hearing the words of Jesus isn't enough. We must put them into action, build them into the very structure and fiber of our lives. If we do this, then no matter how violent the storms of our lives, we will stand firm on a foundation of God's love and protection.

Life Focus

1. Describe a time when your decision was built on "sandy ground." When was it built on "rock"?

2. What event in your life would you like to relive? What would you change about it?

3. What would you like to have etched on your tombstone?

4. In what areas of your life might Jesus say, "I never knew you"?

5. When did you do the "right thing" for the wrong reason?

6. How do you recognize God's presence in your everyday life?

—Diocese of Evansville
  St. Anthony Parish
  Evansville, Indiana

Tenth Sunday of Ordinary Time (A)

Reading I: Hosea 6:3-6
Reading II: Romans 4:18-25
Gospel: Matthew 9:9-13

Scripture Focus

Today's Gospel shows Jesus being rejected by some of the Pharisees. Caught up in observing the Law to the letter, they fail to see the generosity of God's love shown by Jesus. Jesus asked Matthew, a customs collector, to follow him. This man was regarded as a sinner by the Jews and someone to be avoided and scorned. God's mercy is not held from those who appear to be unworthy. In fact, it is precisely to these that God's love reaches out. People are saved by God's graciousness, not by their own efforts or accomplishments. Observance of the law without love for others is not genuine religion.

Life Focus

1. When have you experienced having your life together and being quite independent? When have you experienced a time when you couldn't "do it" alone?

2. The Pharisees complain about Jesus to his disciples instead of going to him directly. Describe a time in your life when you did not have the courage to speak directly to a person you disagreed with or who offended you but complained to others instead.

3. How have you let the law, not love, become a priority in your spiritual life?

—Diocese of Lafayette
  St. Anthony of Padua
  Eunice, Louisiana

(continued)

1. State a time when you closed your mind to Jesus' compassion through your prejudices, hatred or selfishness.

2. Relate a time when you helped others to see God's love in their lives regardless of how sinful they were. Relate a time when you realized that a past event was part of the growing process necessary in getting to know God better.

—Diocese of Lafayette
   Lafayette, Louisiana

Eleventh Sunday of Ordinary Time (A)

Reading I: Exodus 19:2-6
Reading II: Romans 5, 6-11
Gospel: Matthew 9:36—10:8

Scripture Focus

In today's Gospel Jesus sends his disciples out and tells them how to act as his messengers. Jesus' response to the crowds in need of shepherding is to authorize his disciples to extend his own healing. Although here they are told not to preach to non-Jews, later in Matthew's Gospel Jesus will commission his disciples to "go and make disciples of all nations" (28:19). But this will not take place until after the Resurrection. In these early sections of the Gospel, the emphasis is on healing rather than teaching.

Life Focus

1. Speak of a time when it became clear to you that you could make a difference to another. How did you do it?

2. When did you feel overwhelmed by life's demands and didn't know where to seek help?

3. Relate an experience when someone helped you to recognize your worth and value.

—Diocese of Rockville Centre
   The Church of the Good Shepherd
   Holbrook, New York

Twelfth Sunday of Ordinary Time (A)

Reading I: Jeremiah 20:10-13
Reading II: Romans 5:12-15
Gospel: Matthew 10:26-33

Scripture Focus

Today's Gospel deals with persecution and how the disciples were to respond. They were to have complete trust in Jesus. They were to have no fear of those who would threaten their lives. They were to stand strong before the divisions that might come. God, who loved them so much that he counted the hairs on their heads, would not abandon them. Matthew's purpose in emphasizing this care in times of trial comes out of the situation of his community. Many people had rejected the Good News announced by Jesus, and they were rejecting his followers and throwing them out of the synagogues. Through the Gospel, he reminds them that Jesus will be with them through the Spirit as he promised.

Life Focus

1. Describe a time in your life when you were afraid and God seemed far away. What helped you to overcome your fear?

2. When have you allowed someone or something to control you or prevent you from speaking the truth? How did you feel about it afterward?

3. We ask our children to "say no to drugs" and encourage them not to give in to peer pressure. Describe a time when you were swayed by what your peers would say about you.

4. Relate a time when you found it difficult to heed God's command "...do not be afraid of anything."

5. Describe a time when you were "anxious" about an event and it turned out that there was nothing to be concerned about.

—Diocese of Cleveland
  St. Barnabas Church
  Northfield, Ohio

Thirteenth Sunday of Ordinary Time (A)

Reading I: 2 Kings 4:8-11, 14-16
Reading II: Romans 6:3-4, 8-11
Gospel: Matthew 10:37-42

Scripture Focus

Today's Gospel presents the hard choice to be made by those who want to live and spread the Good News. People are not being told to cut off all family ties. But if your family threatens to disown you for following Jesus or for making decisions based upon him, you will have to make a choice. To choose Christ means to follow the path his love marked out. Often that means taking up the cross. Choosing the safe way often leads to self-destruction. In order to find our true identity, we must give ourselves to others, living as Jesus lived.

Life Focus

1. Relate a time when you were made to feel welcome. What did that experience mean to you?

2. Give an example of something in your life over which you cannot relinquish control.

3. Was there ever a time when your values threatened "family ties"? Relate this experience.

—Archdiocese of Cincinnati
  Our Lady of Mercy Parish
  Dayton, Ohio

Fourteenth Sunday of Ordinary Time (A)

Reading I: Zechariah 9:9-10
Reading II: Romans 8:9, 11-13
Gospel: Matthew 11:25-30

Scripture Focus

Jesus praises God's goodness, which brings the truly humble into sharing in the love that joins the Father and the Son. Those who depend only on their own strength and knowledge will never understand God's wisdom and wonderful care. Jesus encourages his listeners to come to him if they are wearied by life. He will share their burdens and restore their sense of balance and peace. People must have the courage and humility to believe in the power of peace and gentleness over aggression and hard-heartedness.

Life Focus

1. What are your childlike qualities? What makes it difficult for you to be childlike?

2. How do you let *life* make you weary?

3. Recall a time in your life when you found peace by turning a certain "burden" over to Jesus.

4. Speak of how you were affected by a person who was strong in conviction but gentle in approach.

—Diocese of Buffalo
  St. Catherine of Siena Parish
  West Seneca, New York

Fifteenth Sunday of Ordinary Time (A)

Reading I: Isaiah 55:10-11
Reading II: Romans 8:18-23
Gospel: Matthew 13:1-23

Scripture Focus

The parable of the sower tells of the fruitfulness of God's creative word. It is a parable about the coming of God's reign. Preaching the kingdom will meet all kinds of obstacles, but in the end it will be successful. As powerful as the word is, however, it needs to be received. We must be willing to listen and to bring the message into our lives. We see this in the way that the disciples, open to God's word, are given insights into "the mysteries of the reign of God."

Life Focus

1. Why do you think God put you on this earth? What harvest is God bringing from your life?

2. What helps or hinders God's ways becoming rooted in your everyday life?

3. When, in the last month, have you felt encouragement and hope in your life?

4. In what way have you enriched God's kingdom?

5. When has personal suffering brought you closer to God?

—Archdiocese of Oklahoma City
  St. John the Baptist Church
  Edmond, Oklahoma

Sixteenth Sunday of Ordinary Time (A)

Reading I: Wisdom 12:13, 16-19
Reading II: Romans 8:26-27
Gospel: Matthew 13:24-43

Scripture Focus

In today's Gospel Jesus tells three parables that describe the kingdom of God. In the first we hear about a field where weeds and wheat grow together. It was difficult to tell the weeds apart from the wheat. To cut or pull the weeds while the wheat was growing would hurt the wheat. When the crop was full grown, however, the weeds could be pulled without endangering the wheat. In the Christian community, we find the same situation—good and bad grow together, and none of us is wise enough to weed out the bad without harming the good. God, the "Master of the Harvest," will make this judgment at the end of time. In the meantime, we must be nonjudgmental and practice patience.

Life Focus

1. Describe a time when you found it difficult to be patient but doing so brought about a positive outcome.

2. Relate an experience in your life when you were glad that someone was patient and gave you additional time.

3. When has a first impression of someone changed from "weed" to "wheat" for you? What would you have missed if you had not taken the time to understand the person more thoroughly?

—Archdiocese of Cincinnati
  St. Francis of Assisi
  Centerville, Ohio

Seventeenth Sunday of Ordinary Time (A)

Reading I: 1 Kings 3:5, 7-12
Reading II: Romans 8:28-30
Gospel: Matthew 13:44-52

Scripture Focus

The Gospel today speaks of true wisdom, a priceless treasure to be sought with all one's heart. In the first comparison Jesus uses, a man discovers a treasure that was so valuable that he "sold all he had and bought the field." In the second comparison a pearl merchant discovers a pearl worth more than all his other possessions. Common to both stories is the marvel of discovering such a prize and giving everything to gain possession of it. The point of both parables is that gaining the treasure of God's saving love is worth any sacrifice.

Life Focus

1. Describe a time when a decision you made seemed right or wise. Name a time when a decision you made seemed to be wrong or unwise. What made the difference in these decisions?

2. Relate an experience when you were able to uncover a "hidden treasure." What helped you to see its value?

3. What in your life now is most valuable to you? How do you find God present in that value?

4. What are you willing to "pay" or "give up" in order to possess what is valuable to you?

5. What about you could be described as being like the "pearl of great price"? What are the gifts that are uncovered by being related to each other as members of the same community?

—Archdiocese of Baltimore
  St. Joseph Catholic Community
  Sykesville, Maryland

Eighteenth Sunday of Ordinary Time (A)

Reading I: Isaiah 55:1-3
Reading II: Romans 8:35, 37-39
Gospel: Matthew 14:13-21

Scripture Focus

Jesus is mourning the death of John the Baptist. But even though he is troubled, Jesus is aware of the needs of those around him. Instead of focusing exclusively on his own needs and concerns, he reaches out to heal others and even to feed a great multitude. This miracle had eucharistic implications for the early Christians. Moreover, he continues to feed the poor and the hungry through his Church. When the disciples suggested that he send the crowd away to "buy some food for themselves," Jesus tells them, "Give them something to eat yourselves." The Christian community is likewise commanded to feed the hungry in its midst. The Eucharist would be an empty ritual if it didn't motivate people to do what Jesus did.

Life Focus

1. Recall a time when you felt mournful, threatened or afraid, but the needs of others took priority.

2. Recall a time when someone helped you in your time of need.

3. Name a time when you helped another who was in material or spiritual need.

4. What are people in your life hungry for? Plan one response.

—Diocese of Bismarck
  Spirit of Life Parish
  Mandan, North Dakota

1. When have you given to another only to find yourself with more than you've given?

2. Relate an experience in your life when you received beyond what you ever hoped for.

—Diocese of Green Bay
  Green Bay, Wisconsin

Nineteenth Sunday of Ordinary Time (A)

Reading I: 1 Kings 19:9, 11-13
Reading II: Romans 9:1-5
Gospel: Matthew 14:22-33

Scripture Focus

Part of the purpose for this Gospel passage was to encourage the community. This account was written fifty years after the Resurrection event. Matthew's audience is suffering opposition, rejection, even persecution. They are beginning to worry that the risen Lord has abandoned them as well. Here Jesus reassures his followers, telling them not to be afraid. Matthew gives special attention to Peter's attempt to walk on water. Peter often acted impulsively. He came to realize his weakness and his need to rely on the Lord for help. Matthew hopes his listeners will come to the same recognition.

Life Focus

1. When has fear overcome trust in your life?

2. Relate an experience when you trusted at first but later began to lose faith.

3. Where do you find courage in your life?

—Diocese of Bismarck
  Bismarck, North Dakota

Twentieth Sunday of Ordinary Time (A)

Reading I: Isaiah 56:6-7
Reading II: Romans 11:13-15, 29-32
Gospel: Matthew 15:21-28

Scripture Focus

The account in this Gospel passage shows that while in the beginning the Good News was preached only to the Jews, there would come a time when all people would be included. Jesus tells his disciples here that his mission is to "the lost sheep of the house of Israel." But at the end of Matthew's Gospel, the Risen Christ will command the apostles to "Go, therefore, and make disciples of *all nations*." This story is a turning point in Jesus' mission. The woman's humility and "great faith" were not to be denied. Faith in the Lord will bring both Jews and Gentiles to healing and salvation.

Life Focus

1. Relate an experience when you felt you were not listened to or when you felt rejected.

2. Relate an experience when you persevered even when you felt ignored.

3. Who are the people who don't get your attention and often aren't included?

4. Relate an experience when your persistence had positive results in a way you did not expect.

—Diocese of Fargo
  Fargo, North Dakota

Twenty-First Sunday of Ordinary Time (A)

Reading I: Isaiah 22:15, 19-23
Reading II: Romans 11:33-36
Gospel: Matthew 16:13-20

Scripture Focus

Matthew is the only evangelist to use the term "Church." Church is an earthly experience of the Kingdom of God. Because Jesus is always with us, the Church can never fail. The keys symbolize opening up doors to truth and wisdom. Giving the "keys of the kingdom" means that authority is being given to teach and make decisions for the Church community, although the extent of that authority is not clear. Authority exists only for the sake of the Church community and its work of proclaiming the Kingdom.

Life Focus

1. When have you felt overwhelmed by responsibility? What did you do about it?

2. When has being part of the Church helped you see life more clearly and act with courage? When has the Church been an obstacle?

3. Relate an experience when you were a "rock" of strength for another person.

4. What qualities do you see in yourself that Jesus saw in Peter?

5. Describe an experience when responsibility was entrusted to you.

6. In your experience, what is it like to be entrusted with a set of keys (to a car, a house, an office or a store)?

7. When did you exercise authority that helped someone open a door to a fuller life?

—Archdiocese of Indianapolis
 Office of Catholic Education
 Indianapolis, Indiana

Twenty-Second Sunday of Ordinary Time (A)

Reading I: Jeremiah 20:7-9
Reading II: Romans 12:1-2
Gospel: Matthew 16:21-27

Scripture Focus

Right after Peter declares that Jesus is the Messiah, Jesus tells of his coming suffering and death. Jesus makes it clear that he is not a powerful military and political leader. For Jesus, the Messiah was not someone to raise Israel to a high place. In fact, Jesus would be rejected by powerful people in both religious and political circles. To further emphasize his message, Jesus continues with the demand of discipleship—selfless love, even if it leads to death, because through the cross comes the glory of resurrection. The reading ends with a bright promise of what lies ahead for those who take Jesus seriously.

Life Focus

1. Name an experience in your daily routine when you willingly gave up something that was in the way of your life's priorities.

2. What doees it mean to you to deny yourself? To take up your cross? To follow Christ?

3. Describe an experience when what seemed to be bad news turned out to be good news.

4. Relate an experience when God's way did not meet your expectations.

—Diocese of Raleigh
 Raleigh, North Carolina

Twenty-Third Sunday of Ordinary Time (A)

Reading I: Ezekiel 33:7-9
Reading II: Romans 13:8-10
Gospel: Matthew 18:15-20

Scripture Focus

In the first reading Ezekiel has been appointed by God as "watchman." Such a person had to keep watch and warn the city of approaching danger. For Ezekiel, personal responsibility is important. The prophet must warn individuals as well as the group. The Gospel reading treats this same theme. Matthew is the only Gospel writer to speak of relationships and responsibilities within the Church. He also offers practical guidelines for fulfilling these responsibilities. Serious community decisions are to be made only after serious prayer. Wisdom must be sought from God and from the presence of Christ in their midst.

Life Focus

1. Relate a time when you hurt someone and the person confronted you about it. How did you feel and how did you respond?

2. Some conflicts are part of any ongoing group. How does your small church community handle conflict?

3. Relate a time when your prayers were answered but not as you expected.

4. When have you experienced the power of prayer through your small community?

—Diocese of Erie
  St. Mark Catholic Center
  Erie, Pennsylvania

Twenty-Fourth Sunday of Ordinary Time (A)

Reading I: Sirach 27:30—28:7
Reading II: Romans 14:7-9
Gospel: Matthew 18:21-35

Scripture Focus

Forgiveness is perhaps one of the greatest challenges individuals and communities face. In this Gospel passage Peter asks Jesus how often he should forgive someone who has wronged him. Jesus' answer—"seventy times seven times" would have meant "no limits" to his listeners. Jesus tells a story about what will happen to those who do not show others the same forgiveness and compassion they have received from God.

Life Focus

1. Who in your life has forgiven you the most?

2. Recall an experience when you held onto a grudge. What was the effect on you?

3. Relate an incident when you forgave someone even though you found it difficult to do so. How do you forgive when you still feel hurt and angry?

4. Recall an experience of forgiving a hurt from the distant past.

5. Describe a time when God's generosity to you made it possible for you to forgive someone else.

—Archdiocese of Los Angeles
  Santa Barbara, California

Twenty-Fifth Sunday of Ordinary Time (A)

Reading I: Isaiah 55:6-9
Reading II: Philippians 1:20-24, 27
Gospel: Matthew 20:1-16

Scripture Focus

The generosity of God continues to be highlighted in today's Gospel. We accept God's gifts and try to live in such a way that shows gratitude and a willingness to imitate God's compassion. The message of the parable of the workers in the vineyard is that God's justice is far beyond our understanding. This parable may have been aimed at those Jewish Christians who resented God's call of the Gentiles to salvation.

Life Focus

1. Describe a time when you were bothered by generosity shown to someone you thought less deserving.

2. Tell of an experience when you were treated better than you thought you deserved.

3. Relate an experience when you were criticized for being generous or forgiving.

4. Describe a time when you felt cheated by someone else's good fortune.

—Archdiocese of Los Angeles
  Los Angeles, California

Twenty-Sixth Sunday of Ordinary Time (A)

Reading I: Ezekiel 18:25-28
Reading II: Philippians 2:1-11
Gospel: Matthew 21:28-32

Scripture Focus

Today's Gospel emphasizes the theme of personal responsibility and accountability. Not only are we to respond with a "yes" to God's call, but we are to carry out the tasks that go with that yes. This parable is set within a series of conflicts Jesus has with the religious authorities. It is Jesus' last week in Jerusalem. The parable is another way of saying, "Not everyone who says to me 'Lord, Lord' will enter the kingdom of heaven, but only the one who does the will of my Father in heaven" (7:21). Our actions and our lives must demonstrate that we truly follow Christ and the message of the Gospel.

Life Focus

1. Relate an experience when you were given a second chance.

2. Describe a time when you were asked to help others but found an excuse not to do it.

3. When have you abused a relationship and had a second chance to renew that relationship? What did you do?

4. When have you had a change of heart?

5. Describe an event or encounter that made you change your behavior or attitude.

—Archdiocese of St. Paul/Minneapolis
  St. Paul, Minnesota

Twenty-Seventh Sunday of Ordinary Time (A)

Reading I: Isaiah 5:1-7
Reading II: Philippians 4:6-9
Gospel: Matthew 21:33-43

Scripture Focus

In this parable of the vineyard, each element of the story has another meaning. The property owner represents God. The first group of slaves represents the prophets. They were sent by God to the people before the exile. The second group represents the prophets sent after the exile. Neither group had any good effect upon the people. Rather they were beaten, killed and stoned. When the owner sent his son (Jesus), they dragged him outside the vineyard (Jerusalem) and killed him also. The listeners to the parable were led to judge the tenants (themselves). Because Jesus had been rejected by the religious authorities, the Kingdom would now be given also to the Gentiles.

Life Focus

1. What or who has helped you during a period of rejection?

2. When have people outside the Church seemed to have more understanding and love than those within?

3. Describe a time when you were so set in your ways that you wouldn't accept repeated invitations to change.

4. Describe a rejection in your life that turned into something positive.

5. How might you miss or reject the good God sends each day?

—Diocese of Steubenville
  Steubenville, Ohio

Twenty-Eighth Sunday of Ordinary Time (A)

Reading I: Isaiah 25:6-10
Reading II: Philippians 4:12-14, 19-20
Gospel: Matthew 22:1-14

Scripture Focus

In the Scriptures, meals are always occasions of sharing of life, memories and intimacy. This simple human experience represents the rich life shared between God and his people. The wedding banquet especially looks to the end time when God and his people will find a final sharing of life with each other. In this parable the first guests invited refuse to come. The king tells his servants to invite everyone they meet, "the bad as well as the good." The Church will never be a perfect community of saintly people. All are invited. The only requirement is to receive the Good News willingly. God doesn't care about the clothes we wear. The point is that to share in the heavenly banquet, one must sincerely be open to the Lord.

Life Focus

1. Relate an experience when you knew you had to change your behavior and you chose not to.

2. Describe an experience when you received an invitation and made up excuses because you didn't want to attend.

3. Who would you rather not be with at the same table? Why?

4. What has the Church done to make you feel part of the community?

5. On what occasion did you feel most out of place in a group?

—Diocese of Helena
  Helena, Montana

44

Twenty-Ninth Sunday of Ordinary Time (A)

Reading I: Isaiah 45:1, 4-6
Reading II: 1 Thessalonians 1:1-5
Gospel: Matthew 22:15-21

Scripture Focus

Matthew makes it very clear that two opposing political groups have united to trap Jesus: If he supported paying taxes to Rome, he would be accused of being a traitor to his "own" people. If he refused such payment, he would be charged with acting against the government. Jesus is not fooled. He turns the situation back at them. It is clear that they have accepted Roman rule because they can produce a Roman coin. It belongs to Caesar; it has his image and inscription on it. So Jesus says if it belongs to him give it to him, but "give to God what is God's." He is telling them that there is a Kingdom higher than that of Caesar. All people are made in the image of God. They belong to God, and Jesus calls them to give their lives to God, not to earthly concerns.

Life Focus

1. Relate an experience when you felt pressured into making a decision contrary to your principles.

2. Describe an experience of being caught in a no-win situation with family, at work or in society.

3. What belongs only to God in your life?

—Diocese of Rockville Centre
 Rockville Centre, New York

Thirtieth Sunday of Ordinary Time (A)

Reading I: Exodus 22:20-26
Reading II: 1 Thessalonians 1:5-10
Gospel: Matthew 22:34-40

Scripture Focus

Sometimes we hear people speak of the God of the Old Testament as a harsh judge, while the God of the New Testament is a loving and compassionate God. But there is only one God. Today's first reading from the Book of Exodus deals with the Ten Commandments and some specific ways they are to be lived and understood. These commandments are not burdensome and oppressive. In fact, they are essential if humankind is to live a free civilized life. They will ensure our happiness. In the Gospel Jesus' enemies try once again to trip him up. They think he will speak against the Law of Moses. But Jesus agrees that the greatest commandment is to love God with one's whole being, with one's heart and mind and soul. The second commandment, "You shall love your neighbor as yourself," follows from and completes the first. This twofold command sums up the Law of Moses and the teachings of all the Hebrew prophets.

Life Focus

1. How was it tough to love someone this week?

2. From your personal experience, what keeps you from loving God, your neighbor or yourself? Of the three, which for you is the hardest to love?

3. How have you shown concern for another in a simple way this week?

4. What/who helps you stay centered on what really counts in life?

5. Relate an experience when you treated another as you would want to be treated.

—Archdiocese of St. Louis, Missouri
 Diocese of Springfield, Illinois

Thirty-First Sunday of Ordinary Time (A)

Reading I: Malachi 1:14; 2:2, 8-10
Reading II: 1 Thessalonians 2:7-9, 13
Gospel: Matthew 23:1-12

Scripture Focus

In today's Gospel Jesus comes right out and accuses scribes and Pharisees, the religious leaders, of being false. Some Pharisees, who were supposed to be role models for the people, taught one thing but lived in another way. Jesus told the disciples to respect the Pharisees' positions as successors of Moses and to take their teachings seriously. But the disciples were not to follow the Pharisees' example. Jesus makes it clear to his followers that they must honor and respect God instead of being overly concerned about their own importance and power. They were called to serve others, not be applauded by them.

Life Focus

1. Are you aware of any instances in your life when the image you presented to others was not borne out by your actions? How did you feel? What did you learn? What caused you to become aware that you were untrue? What change happened?

2. Describe a time when you felt you were better than another person and refused to relate with them in any way (poor neighborhood, less money, a church with minorities, ethnic or lower social positions).

3. Give an example of a leader you know who doesn't have to be important in everyone's eyes but tries to be of service to others.

4. Describe a time when someone did something special for you without letting you know who it was.

5. Relate an experience when you felt too proud to be with a person who might embarrass you, or when you didn't want to do a job you considered beneath you.

—Archdiocese of Indianapolis
  St. Joan of Arc Church
  Indianapolis, Indiana

Thirty-Second Sunday of Ordinary Time (A)

Reading I: Wisdom 6:12-16
Reading II: 1 Thessalonians 4:13-18
Gospel: Matthew 25:1-13

Scripture Focus

Today's Gospel passage is part of Jesus' talk on the end time, when the world we know will end and God's Kingdom will come completely. Jesus tells a parable that urges people to be ready for this great event, the eternal wedding reception. The delayed arrival of the groom is the delayed Second Coming of Jesus. People must not be lulled into carelessness, into thinking that it will never happen. It will—and we do not know when. The theme of this parable is that the wise are prepared to complete their task. The oil in today's passage is the good works done for others. We must be prepared by living according to the gospel, doing good for others.

Life Focus

1. Tell of a time when you missed out on a good thing because you were not prepared.

2. What helps you prepare your "light" for Christ's coming?

3. What has happened to help you remain faithful to your faith journey?

—Diocese of Evansville
  Evansville, Indiana

Thirty-Third Sunday of Ordinary Time (A)

Reading I: Proverbs 31:10-13, 19-20, 30-31
Reading II: 1 Thessalonians 5:1-6
Gospel: Matthew 25:14-30

Scripture Focus

As we approach the end of the liturgical year, our attention is drawn more and more to the end of our lives and the accounting we must give for our use of God's gifts. Jesus' parable speaks for itself. The faithful servants are generously rewarded because they were responsible and used what was given to them. Our relationship with God is not a cold business deal. But God expects us to show gratitude for the gifts given us and for God's confidence in our mature sense of responsibility by using these talents.

Life Focus

1. What are the most important gifts you have been given?

2. For one or two of the most important gifts, describe how you are showing gratitude for them.

3. If your life ended today, what from your life would you be most pleased to set before God?

4. For what gifts do you need to show more gratitude? How will you do so this week?

—Diocese of Pittsburgh
  St. Margaret Church
  Pittsburgh, Pennsylvania

Solemnity of Christ the King (A)

Reading I: Ezekiel 34:11-12, 15-17
Reading II: 1 Corinthians 15:20-26, 28
Gospel: Matthew 25:31-46

Scripture Focus

Today's description of the last judgment goes further than any other. This final judgment determines what counts in the end. It is not success or how perfectly a person has developed. In the end, the judgment is about love for the poorest, the no-accounts, the ones easy to miss. It is not about doing good or charitable things for a cause or out of a sense of duty. What counts is doing real practical good out of genuine love. Jesus tells us that when we do this, we are serving Jesus himself.

Life Focus

1. When have you felt "left out" and when have you felt accepted?

2. When this week did you see another hungry, naked, thirsty, sick, in prison? How did you respond?

3. Describe a time when helping others was your way of living this Gospel.

4. As a Church, whom do we easily pass by?

—Archdiocese of Toronto
  Toronto, Ontario, Canada

Commentaries and Questions for Cycle B

First Sunday of Advent (B)

Reading I: Isaiah 63:16-17, 19; 64:2-7
Reading II: 1 Corinthians 1:3-9
Gospel: Mark 13:33-37

Scripture Focus

Advent literally means "coming." This coming refers to the first coming of Jesus as a baby in Nazareth, his coming into the hearts of faithful Christians throughout the ages and his final coming in glory at the end of the world. Christians in the first century looked for Christ to return soon to establish once and for all God's reign of justice, peace and love. The parable we hear in Mark's Gospel encouraged the early Christians not to grow careless. Advent is a time of joyful expectation. Jesus will come again. He will not forget his own. Keep looking!

Life Focus

1. Describe an experience that continually helps you renew hope in your life.

2. How do you show hope in your daily life?

3. Relate a recent experience of God's presence. How were you able to find God in the experience?

4. Relate an experience when not being alert put you in danger. How did you find God in that experience?

5. What ways do you use to bring God into your life every day?

—Diocese of Albany
   Albany, New York

Second Sunday of Advent (B)

Reading I: Isaiah 40:1-5, 9-11
Reading II: 2 Peter 3:8-14
Gospel: Mark 1:1-8

Scripture Focus

Advent is a season of fresh beginnings. The writer of Second Isaiah gives people a message of hope and comfort. The exiles will return to Jerusalem on a straight and level road. Isaiah proclaims the good news that God is always faithful, a God of both power and tenderness. Mark begins the account of the Good News (the meaning of the word *gospel*). Jesus, God's son sent to heal us and lead us home, is himself the Good News. Mark begins by telling us about John the Baptist, the herald of the good news of Jesus' coming. Today, we are called to be heralds of this same Good News. We announce to a hurting world that Jesus Christ has experienced the worst we face and has come through it.

Life Focus

1. Relate an experience when someone helped you to see your need to change.

2. Describe an experience when you prepared for a special someone coming into your life.

3. How are you preparing for Christ's coming?

4. Describe a time you helped make someone's pathway easier.

5. Describe a time when someone brought you news that changed your life.

—Archdiocese of New Orleans
   New Orleans, Louisiana

Third Sunday of Advent (B)

Reading I: Isaiah 61:1-2, 10-11
Reading II: 1 Thessalonians 5:16-24
Gospel: John 1:6-8, 19-28

Scripture Focus

In this Gospel, John the Baptist saw his role clearly. At the time John was writing his Gospel, followers of John the Baptist were claiming that he, not Jesus, was the Messiah. So here the Gospel writer emphasizes that John the Baptist saw himself as one to prepare the way for the Messiah. He is not the Messiah nor any of the others they suggest. He is just "a voice in the desert" preparing the way for the Lord. His baptism is a simple water rite, unlike Jesus' baptism in the Holy Spirit. John the Baptist proclaims the Good News of Jesus' coming and prepares people's hearts for that event.

Life Focus

1. How do you answer the question "Who are you?"

2. Describe a time when something insignificant to others meant a lot to you.

3. Who is your prophet? How did this prophet affect your life?

4. What potholes do you find on your path to Jesus?

5. Who has recently helped you to have faith?

—Diocese of Evansville
   St. Anthony Parish
   Evansville, Indiana

Fourth Sunday of Advent (B)

Reading I: 2 Samuel 7:1-5, 8-11, 16
Reading II: Romans 16:25-27
Gospel: Luke 1:26-38

Scripture Focus

In today's reading from Second Samuel, David is determined to build a house for God. But the prophet Nathan tells him that instead *God* would build a royal house, a dynasty, for him. Even after the failure of David's descendants as kings, the Jews believed that the Messiah would come from the line of David. In today's passage from Luke's Gospel, we discover that the house the Lord settles on is the womb of the young woman Mary. The angel tells Mary that her child will be "Son of the Most High. The Lord God will give him the throne of David his father. He will rule over the house of Jacob forever and his reign will be without end." This announcement in the Gospel again shows that God approaches us with love first.

Life Focus

1. What experiences in your life have led you to accept things at face value?

2. Relate an experience when you were expected to do something that you thought would be impossible.

3. Speak of a time when you felt troubled or fearful.

4. When has someone cared for you before you could ever respond?

—Archdiocese of San Antonio
   San Antonio, Texas

(continued)

1. A Navajo woman carrying a child has an awareness of God's presence around her, above her, below her and within her. Do you have this same awareness of God's presence in you?

2. A Navajo hogan is a six- to eight-sided traditional ceremonial hut with an earth floor. It symbolizes the spiritual prayer and life of the Navajo Indian. Is your life, like a hogan, held firm with love and respect for all life, and open to receive and share with others?

—Diocese of Gallup, New Mexico
  Our Lady of Fatima Parish
  Chinle, Arizona

Solemnity of Christmas

(See Cycle A, pages 7-9.)

Feast of the Holy Family (B)

Reading I: Sirach 3:2-6, 12-14
Reading II: Colossians 3:12-21
Gospel: Luke 2:22-40

Scripture Focus

The Gospel reading begins with the simple scene of a devout Jewish family obeying the Law. The holy man Simeon then meets them and says that this child will fulfill the hopes of Israel. Not only that, he will be a "revealing light to the Gentiles." One of Luke's dominant themes is salvation for everyone, Gentiles as well as Jews. This simple and strong description of the Holy Family concludes with their return home to ordinary daily life in a small village.

Life Focus

1. In what way(s) does your family express the love of God to each other? To others outside the family? Where does your family need healing?

2. Reflect a time or event(s) in your childhood that you now realize deepened your faith.

3. In your life, what families have had an effect on you? How?

—Diocese of Bismarck
  Spirit of Life Parish
  Mandan, North Dakota

1. Relate a time when your choice put you at odds with your family or friends.

2. Tell of an experience when you, like Simeon, could grasp the value of another person and the good that person could bring about.

—Diocese of Buffalo
  St. Catherine of Siena Parish
  West Seneca, New York

Solemnity of Epiphany

(See Cycle A, page 10.)

Baptism of the Lord (B)

Reading I: Isaiah 42:1-4, 6-7
Reading II: Acts 10:34-38
Gospel: Mark 1:7-11

Scripture Focus

The Christmas season comes to an end with this feast of the Lord's baptism. God reveals his son to us as Jesus begins his work. The creation account in Genesis tells us that the spirit hovered over the waters and brought forth the world out of chaos. In the account of the baptism, Jesus comes up out of the water and the spirit descends upon him as a sign of God's favor. A new world is created in Christ.

Life Focus

1. In what ways and/or by whom have you been affirmed since you were baptized?

2. Recall a time when you felt that your life began anew.

3. Recall a time when you were chosen to do something special. What effect did it have in your life?

4. How have you been able to help this new world come about this last week?

—Diocese of Cleveland
Cleveland, Ohio

First Sunday of Lent (B)

Reading I: Genesis 9:8-15
Reading II: 1 Peter 3:18-22
Gospel: Mark 1:12-15

Scripture Focus

On this first Sunday of Lent, we hear Mark's version of Jesus being tempted in the desert. Jesus begins with this confrontation with evil. The rest of his life and work will continue this great battle: casting out demons, healing, struggling for the truth against corrupt leaders and even the blindness of his own disciples. Through it all, he proclaims the good news that the time of God's reign is now. God's truth and love is stronger than distortion and injustice. Believe the good news and it can change your life.

Life Focus

1. Relate an experience when you were "tested."

2. Describe a time when you were challenged to confront a weakness in your life.

3. Talk about an obstacle in the recent past that could be keeping you from becoming a better person. What might such an obstacle be in the weeks ahead?

4. Explain how you deal with failures in your life.

—Diocese of Great Falls
Billings, Montana

Second Sunday of Lent (B)

Reading I: Genesis 22:1-2; 9:10-13, 15-18
Reading II: Romans 8:31-34
Gospel: Mark 9:2-10

Scripture Focus

Throughout Mark's Gospel, we hear the question
"Who is Jesus?" In the transfiguration, we hear the
clearest answer. But this foreshadowing of the
Resurrection comes between two predictions of
suffering and rejection. Even Jesus' closest apostles
fail to understand what Jesus means by "rising from
the dead," and they do not want to hear his predictions
of his Passion. But Mark makes it clear to his audience
that resurrection can only be understood in the
mystery of suffering and dying.

Life Focus

1. Relate an experience when a person turned out to be
much more than you expected.

2. Reflect on an experience of great beauty, wisdom or
courage in suffering that has stayed with you
afterward and continues to move you.

3. Name someone who dealt with a necessary struggle
and suffering instead of running away. How did this
affect you?

4. Describe an experience of beauty or love that
captured your attention.

—Diocese of Camden
  Camden, New Jersey

Third Sunday of Lent (B)

Reading I: Exodus 20:1-17
Reading II: 1 Corinthians 1:22-25
Gospel: John 2:13-25

Scripture Focus

In John's Gospel one of the first things Jesus does as
he begins his work is to drive the money-changers out
of the temple. His life and his work that follows are
summed up in the statement, "Zeal for my Father's
house consumes me." Everything Jesus does is based
on the loving relationship he has with his Father. Here
his actions express his desire to purify the
relationship of the children of Israel with the God who
called them into covenant. Throughout John's Gospel,
Jesus will invite others into the relationship he shares
with the Father.

Life Focus

1. When have you felt so strongly about a person or
cause that you acted on his/her/its behalf?

2. Relate a time when something you valued deeply
was not respected, especially by members of your
family or church. How did you deal with that?

3. Speak of an experience when you were upset with
the Church. How did you deal with it?

4. What are the choices and priorities you are making
today that keep your life a marketplace?

5. What actions and attributes need to die in you so
you can come to Easter?

—Archdiocese of St. Louis
  St. Louis, Missouri

Fourth Sunday of Lent

Reading I: 2 Chronicles 36:14-17, 19-23
Reading II: Ephesians 2:4-10
Gospel: John 3:14-21

Scripture Focus

When John speaks of Jesus being lifted up on the cross, he refers to more than Jesus' death. This lifting up is the whole sweep of Jesus coming from and returning to his father: life, death, being raised from the tomb, being exalted over the whole world. The reference to the serpent Moses raised in the desert is the story we hear in our first reading. The Israelites, bitten by serpents as a result of their grumbling in the desert, are cured by looking on the image of their woundedness. In the same way, Jesus has taken on our humanity and will bring healing and eternal life through his death and glorification. The very life and love of God can be seen and touched in the only Son, lifted up for us.

Life Focus

1. Describe a time when you felt yourself being drawn from anxiety, fear, hurt, anger, etc., because someone didn't leave you to carry these alone.

2. Relate a recent experience when you felt light and/or love.

3. Give one experience when you believed in God's love for you.

4. In the next two weeks, what would help you become more alive?

—Archdiocese of Hartford
 Hartford, Connecticut

Fifth Sunday of Lent (B)

Reading I: Jeremiah 31:31-34
Reading II: Hebrews 5:7-9
Gospel: John 12:20-33

Scripture Focus

In today's Gospel Jesus speaks of real resurrection. And he tells his followers that the only way to come to this life of glory is by dying. The image of the grain of wheat offers a powerful example of this reality. A single seed is limited and alone. But if the seed dies to its present state, it will grow into a stalk filled with seeds. The message for us is that the present is good, but because Christ has brought an end to death through his own death and resurrection, we can look forward to a future that will be far more than our limited lives here and now.

Life Focus

1. Relate a time when you lost out but later were strengthened by this experience.

2. Describe an experience in your life when seeds fell fruitlessly but later blossomed.

3. What struggles have you let go of? What struggles did you surrender to?

4. Whose life and struggles encourage you?

—Diocese of Madison
 Madison, Wisconsin

Passion/Palm Sunday (B)

Reading I: Isaiah 50:4-7
Reading II: Philippians 2:6-11
Gospel: Mark 14:1—15:47

Scripture Focus

Mark's Gospel, more than the other Gospels, shows the human struggle and suffering of Jesus. Jesus seems to feel abandoned at the worst point. Mark's community, undergoing persecution, needed to make sense of the suffering in their lives. They needed to discover who Jesus was as Messiah. Throughout the Gospel, we get hints and glimpses of who Jesus is. Today we come to the story of the Passion itself. Mark finally answers the question of who Jesus is only at the end, when the centurion proclaims: "Clearly this man was the Son of God." Jesus' identity as Messiah is only fully revealed when he dies on the cross.

Life Focus

1. Recall a time when life didn't make sense at all. What, if anything, kept you trusting?

2. Remember a time when you helped someone who was carrying a heavy burden.

3. Recall a time in your life when someone helped you through a burdensome time.

4. Peter denied Jesus threefold. Recall a time when you found it hard to take a stand for the values of Christ.

—Diocese of Madison
  St. Bernard Parish
  Middleton, Wisconsin

1. Describe a personal experience of suffering. Was God there for you? How?

2. When were you treated unfairly and you felt you didn't deserve it?

3. Recalling Judas' betrayal, name a time you remained faithful to someone or something through difficulty.

—Diocese of La Crosse
  La Crosse, Wisconsin

Triduum

(See Cycle A, pages 18-21.)

Easter Sunday

(See Cycle A, page 22.)

Second Sunday of Easter (B)

Reading I: Acts 4:32-35
Reading II: 1 John 5:1-6
Gospel: John 20:19-31

Scripture Focus

Thomas, who was absent when Jesus first appeared to the apostles in the locked upper room, refused to believe that the Lord had risen. Now, Jesus speaks to Thomas and tells him, "Examine my hands, put your finger into the wound in my side, do not persist in your unbelief but believe." Thomas moves from unbelief to belief. Thomas saw and believed and new life was given to him. We who have not seen and have believed have also been given new life by God. The Spirit's presence within those who believe testifies that Jesus is the Son of God.

Life Focus

1. Relate an experience when you requested proof of something that you should not have doubted.

2. When has Jesus come to you "through locked doors" and you tried not to let him in?

3. Describe an unexpected experience in your life that made you more aware of God's presence.

—Diocese of Crookston
St. Joseph Catholic Church
Bagley, Minnesota

1. Describe how you felt when you had to trust another person.

2. Share a time when you felt doubt and abandonment. How was God present or not present for you?

3. When have you forgiven others? What happened when you were unable/unwilling to?

4. What don't you forgive easily in yourself? What prevents you from forgiving yourself?

—Archdiocese of San Francisco
San Francisco, California

1. Describe an experience in your life when you found it hard to forgive. What were your difficulties in coming to forgiveness?

2. What specific differences would take place in your life this week if you seriously believe that Jesus Christ actually has been raised from the dead?

—Diocese of Port Pirie
Whyalla West Parish-Our Lady Help of Christians Church
Whyalla Stuart, Australia

Third Sunday of Easter (B)

Reading I: Acts 3:13-15, 17-19
Reading II: 1 John 2:1-5
Gospel: Luke 24:35-48

Scripture Focus

In today's Gospel Jesus appears among the disciples. Even though they have heard that he appeared to Simon and to the disciples on the road to Emmaus, they think he is a ghost. At Jesus' invitation to touch him, to look at his wounds, they are filled with joy, but they do not completely believe. Only his eating in their presence convinces them that he is indeed the risen Lord. As he had done on the road, he opens their minds to the Scriptures. After he has done this, he sends them to share the Good News with others.

Life Focus

1. Speak of your life as a mixture of belief and lack of faith at the same time.

2. Relate an experience that brought peace to your life in the middle of difficulties.

3. Who do you know who lives and acts as if Christ is truly alive? How does this person affect you?

—Diocese of Port Pirie
  Whyalla West Parish-Our Lady Help of Christians Church
  Whyalla Stuart, Australia

Fourth Sunday of Easter (B)

Reading I: Acts 4:8-12
Reading II: 1 John 3:1-2
Gospel: John 10:11-18

Scripture Focus

During the Easter season, we look at how Jesus' Resurrection continues to affect people's lives. In the first reading from Acts, Peter heals a cripple in the manner and power of Jesus. In John's Gospel Jesus describes himself as a *good* shepherd. He knows his sheep by name; he knows their habits and traits. His sheep know him. His love for them is so great that he freely lays down his life for them. People who know each other in the deep way described in this passage share their thoughts, feelings and will. They become one heart and one mind. Each has no life without the other. Jesus and his Father know each other in that way. Now Jesus tells his followers that they too have a share in this depth and intimacy.

Life Focus

1. Describe a fearful or hurting situation when someone was there for you.

2. Have you allowed the people in your life to come to know you, as Jesus knows his sheep? What gets in the way?

3. Reflect on a life situation in which God may have been trying to get a message through to you.

—Diocese of San Diego
  San Diego, California

(continued)

1. Was there a time when you felt lost and needed someone to find you?

2. Relate a time when you reached out to someone who was "lost."

3. What will it cost you to be a true shepherd?

—Diocese of Venice
   Fort Meyers, Florida

1. Relate the ways you are a good shepherd to your family and community.

2. What experience can you relate that was motivated more by love than money or reward?

—Diocese of Port Pirie
   Whyalla West Parish-Our Lady Help of Christians Church
   Whyalla Stuart, Australia

Fifth Sunday of Easter (B)

Reading I: Acts 9:26-31
Reading II: 1 John 3:18-24
Gospel: John 15:1-8

Scripture Focus

John speaks of Jesus doing the work of the Father. He knows the love and concern of the Father. The image of the vine and the branches reveals the union between Jesus and us. Together the vine, Jesus, and the branches, his disciples, bear much fruit. The One who causes to grow, prunes and trims is the Father. The works of Jesus become part of the disciple. We are to live as Jesus lived, to love as he loved. Jesus not only revealed God's love for us, he gave evidence of this love "by laying down his life for us." To be followers of Jesus we must give witness to him by our words and deeds.

Life Focus

1. What do you need to prune in your life?

2. What nourishment do you need to help you increase your yield?

3. Speak of a time when you were able to do more than your limitations allowed because of your communion with Christ.

4. In your experience, where is there a real bond between you and the other people of the Church? Where is that unity missing? How will you strengthen those bonds?

—Diocese of Port Pirie
   Whyalla West Parish-Our Lady Help of Christians Church
   Whyalla Stuart, Australia

Sixth Sunday of Easter (B)

Reading I: Acts 10:25-26, 34-35, 44-48
Reading II: 1 John 4:7-10
Gospel: John 15:9-17

Scripture Focus

In today's Gospel Jesus makes it clear that his leaving is not everything. He promises that his disciples will live on in his love by keeping the commandments. He promises them joy in their continued union, and he is glad to call them friends. Jesus reminds them that he has made known to them all that he heard from the Father. The challenge for them is to go forward and bear fruit by loving one another. God sent his only Son that "we might have life through him." Others are to have life through us. In the reading from Acts, Peter comes to realize that this gift is to be extended to uncircumcised Gentiles as well as Jews. Anyone who reverences God and acts according to God's will is acceptable to God.

Life Focus

1. As you reflect on Jesus calling you his friend, what thoughts and feelings come to you? How might you respond this week?

2. When in the last two weeks did you recognize God's love in your life?

3. What does it mean in your life to love yourself? What things in you hinder you from loving yourself?

4. Which people do you find most difficult to notice and be concerned about?

—Diocese of Port Pirie
   Whyalla West Parish-Our Lady Help of Christians Church
   Whyalla Stuart, Australia

1. Who has helped you to understand God a little more? How has that happened?

—Archdiocese of New York
   New York, New York

Seventh Sunday of Easter (B)

Reading I: Acts 1:15-17, 20-26
Reading II: 1 John 4:11-16
Gospel: John 17:11-19

Scripture Focus

During his life, Jesus revealed to his followers what God was like. By his words and deeds he taught them. They were faithful to him and to the truth. He kept them from departing from the truth. He also kept them from getting hurt. As Jesus prepares to return to the Father, he asks the Father to keep them faithful to the truth and to witness to all that Jesus said and did. Believers are to continue the words and works of Jesus. Jesus prays that they may be one in the same way he and his Father are one. This unity of the disciples with each other will be the way the world will come to believe.

Life Focus

1. In your experience, what are the specific ways in which you experience real mutual belonging and care for each other in the parish? How can these ties be strengthened?

2. Reflect on a time when you found it easier to have a faith in God without seeking a commitment to the people of the Church.

3. What are some of the values of your faith community that you can show to the world? How can you do it this week?

—Diocese of Port Pirie
   Whyalla West Parish-Our Lady Help of Christians Church
   Whyalla Stuart, Australia

1. Describe an experience when you eventually found you were not alone after all.

—Archdiocese of New York
   New York, New York

59

Body and Blood of Christ (B)

Reading I: Exodus 24:3-8
Reading II: Hebrews 9:11-15
Gospel: Mark 14:12-16, 22-26

Scripture Focus

For Mark, the Last Supper consciously recalls the Passover meal that celebrated God's leading the Jewish people from slavery in Egypt to their own country. In Jesus, a new covenant is formed between God and the people. Jesus uses the Passover symbols of blessing the bread and wine and passing them around. But he goes beyond this to claim the bread as his body and the wine as his blood. As the Letter to the Hebrews explains, Jesus shed his own blood to cleanse us from our sins. We come to worship the living God by heeding and doing everything God has called us to do. In the "blood of the covenant," a new community is formed. The early Christians celebrated the Eucharist with joy. They anticipated the heavenly banquet they would share with Christ and each other.

Life Focus

1. Speak of an experience from your life when you were willing to sacrifice for others as Jesus did for us.

2. Identify something that you are not able to sacrifice willingly.

3. Recall a time when you prepared a special meal. What was the occasion? What were your feelings?

4. Imagine not being able to receive the Eucharist. How would this affect you?

5. After celebrating the first Eucharist, Jesus and his friends went out singing songs of praise. In what ways do you like to praise God?

—Archdiocese of New Orleans
  Resurrection of Our Lord Church
  New Orleans, Louisiana

Trinity Sunday (B)

Reading I: Deuteronomy 4:32-34, 39-40
Reading II: Romans 8:14-17
Gospel: Matthew 28:16-20

Scripture Focus

Matthew tells us that the apostles now recognize Jesus in his risen life and they worship him. Jesus drew near to them as he always draws near to humankind. Having formed them as his disciples, he now sends them forth in turn to make disciples of *all nations*. They are to baptize people in such a way that they will be seen as sons and daughters of God. The trinity—Father, Son and Holy Spirit—describes an experience of the one, true God who creates, liberates and makes holy. Into this God, a community of persons, we are plunged by our Baptism.

Life Focus

1. How are you answering Jesus' call to be a disciple?

2. Christ sends us to all peoples. Where do you find yourself too narrow in your approach to people, too limited by your upbringing?

3. Describe a time when you "entertained doubts" about God.

—Diocese of Albany
  St. Patrick Parish
  Albany, New York

1. Tell of an experience when you felt your life was put together well.

2. Relate an experience of struggling with something you felt was too much for you. How did you resolve it?

3. How has your view about God changed during your lifetime? What caused the change?

—Archdiocese of New York
  New York, New York

Second Sunday of Ordinary Time (B)

Reading I: 1 Samuel 3:3-10, 19
Reading II: 1 Corinthians 6:13-15, 17-20
Gospel: John 1:35-42

Scripture Focus

John the Baptist's role is to identify Jesus as the Lamb of God, who will forgive the sins of the world. This statement recognizes Jesus' importance and leads John's disciples to leave him to follow Jesus, the Son of God. In this short section of the Gospel, much is said about openness, for example, the ability to accept the word about Jesus and letting one's heart be moved.

Life Focus

1. Relate an experience when you met someone who helped you change your priorities, values or outlook.

2. How has someone else's willingness to try something new or to meet a new person changed you?

3. Relate a time when you were stubborn about a new experience but eventually realized its value.

4. What are you really looking for in your life?

—Diocese of Brooklyn
  Brooklyn, New York

Third Sunday of Ordinary Time (B)

Reading I: Jonah 3:1-5, 10
Reading II: 1 Corinthians 7:29-31
Gospel: Mark 1:14-20

Scripture Focus

Today's passage begins Jesus' preaching and is the core message of everything he will say later. To repent means to change one's mind, to completely change one's attitude from self-centeredness to God-centeredness. It suggests a total change in one's life. We see an example of this in Jesus' call to his first followers and their response. Simon and Andrew set aside what has been their life's work to follow Jesus. Their immediate response to accept Jesus' call testifies to their recognizing him as their leader. James and John, too, abandon work and father to follow Jesus. Believing in the gospel means a personal attachment to the person of Jesus and going with him on his way.

Life Focus

1. Relate an experience when you were drawn to someone and it changed your life.

2. Describe a change in your life which resulted from another's call.

3. When did you find it necessary to leave someone or something behind in order to make a change?

4. Describe an experience in your life when you have felt compelled to make a significant change.

5. Name a time when you had a change of heart or mind.

—Archdiocese of Omaha
  Omaha, Nebraska

Fourth Sunday of Ordinary Time (B)

Reading I: Deuteronomy 18:15-20
Reading II: 1 Corinthians 7:32-35
Gospel: Mark 1:21-28

Scripture Focus

The most important question Mark's Gospel asks is, "Who is Jesus?" Jesus speaks with authority, and people were stunned with the knowledge of the Scriptures Jesus displayed. Beyond this, his very presence changes situations. When he drives out the evil spirit, the crowd doesn't understand when the shrieking demon calls him by name—"the holy one of God." They discuss the power over evil and go out to spread the news throughout all of Galilee, but they keep asking, "Who is he?" For them and for us, it's more important to let the holy presence and authority of Jesus into the situations of our lives and of our world than to look for verbal answers and definitions of who Jesus is.

Life Focus

1. When has someone's presence brought change in your life? Was it negative or positive?

2. Relate an experience when God might be working to overcome an evil situation.

3. Name an action you can take this week to give God greater influence in your life.

—Archdiocese of Atlanta
  Atlanta, Georgia

Fifth Sunday of Ordinary Time (B)

Reading I: Job 7:1-4, 6-7
Reading II: 1 Corinthians 9:16-19, 22-23
Gospel: Mark 1:29-39

Scripture Focus

Jesus cures Simon's mother-in-law. She is so completely cured, she waits on them immediately. Jesus continues all kinds of cures and expels all kinds of demons as the whole town gathers at the house. But Jesus refuses to be locked into an identity as a wonder-worker. He tells his closest disciples that his mission is to preach the good news that the reign of God is at hand. The cures he works are only a sign of God's reign breaking into the here and now.

Life Focus

1. When have you felt boxed-in by someone else's expectations and image of you?

2. Name an event in your life when God's intervention had a more far-reaching effect than you imagined.

3. Relate an experience when you had to withdraw for a period of prayer and reflection in order to be reenergized.

4. Where do you find strength for your call in life?

—Diocese of Orange
  Orange, California

Sixth Sunday of Ordinary Time (B)

Reading I: Leviticus 13:1-2, 44-46
Reading II: 1 Corinthians 10:31—11:1
Gospel: Mark 1:40-45

Scripture Focus

According to Jewish law, lepers were considered unclean and outcasts from society. Yet in today's Gospel, Jesus immediately responds to a leper's request for healing. Jesus had great respect for the Law of Moses so he told the leper to fulfill the cleansing requirements by offering sacrifice and appearing before the priest. Jesus orders him to tell no one who had cured him, but the leper ignores Jesus' command and tells everyone what happened. In spite of the growing difficulties of his ministry, Jesus continues healing and preaching. He was able to proceed because people had faith in him.

Life Focus

1. Jesus reaches out to these outcasts. What groups do you have the most difficulty accepting?

2. Relate a time when you were moved with compassion toward someone who was considered "unclean."

3. Describe a time when you recognized and accepted another person's ability to help you.

4. Tell of a time when you were or were not able to keep good news to yourself.

—Diocese of Helena
  St. Richard Parish
  Columbia Falls, Montana

Seventh Sunday of Ordinary Time (B)

Reading I: Isaiah 43:18-19, 21-22, 24-25
Reading II: 2 Corinthians 1:18-22
Gospel: Mark 2:1-12

Scripture Focus

On the surface this seems to be the story of an ordinary healing miracle by Jesus. But beneath the physical cure is the extraordinary act of forgiveness of sins. Only God can forgive sin. Jesus, having the spirit of God upon him and being the Holy One of God, is able to forgive sin. His cure of the man's lameness dramatizes the greater cure of the soul. Through this action Jesus declares that "...the Son of Man has the authority to forgive sins." It would have been easy merely to say, "your sins are forgiven"; the physical cure gave public evidence of Jesus' power over the forces of evil.

Life Focus

1. What helps me realize God's continuous love and forgiveness?

2. When have you experienced forgiveness? When have you forgiven another?

—Archdiocese of Anchorage
  Friends of Jesus Prayer Group
  Anchorage, Alaska

(continued)

1. Recall a time when you made a special effort to help someone in difficulty. How did you make "a hole in the roof" and bring that person healing?

2. What generally keeps you from *forgetting* a hurt even after you have forgiven the offender?

3. Remember a time when you were forgiven for a wrong you did. Explain how the forgiveness also brought you healing in mind and heart.

4. When you have hurt someone, what most often prevents you from asking for forgiveness immediately? How have you learned to deal with that?

—Diocese of El Obeid
 El Obeid, Sudan

Eighth Sunday of Ordinary Time (B)

Reading I: Hosea 2:16, 17, 21-22
Reading II: 2 Corinthians 3:1-6
Gospel: Mark 2:18-22

Scripture Focus

A series of sayings emphasizes that with Jesus a new age has dawned. It is the time of the "bridegroom," a time for replacing the whole cloth, a time for new wine and new wineskins. These images stress that the new age of salvation is present in Jesus and new things are possible. Jesus' ministry brought in a totally new era, calling for a new life-style. The images of the cloak and the wineskins stress the incompatibility of the new with the old. "Band-Aid" measures will not work: A brand new cloak and fresh wineskins are required.

Life Focus

1. Describe a time in your life when you were or were not open to a new way of doing something.

2. What in your life is new? What is the old that you have let go of?

3. How are you challenged today to reach to new ways of understanding?

4. Have the following statements described you at any time? Have you:
   • been native to your neighborhood?
   • been part of the established culture?
   • not fit in with those people living around you?
   • had beliefs/ideas that are not welcomed by others?

5. When were you open to another's ideas or feelings that were contrary to yours?

6. Are you open to risking new ways to live out Jesus' command to love one another? How?

—Diocese of Providence
 St. Lucy Church
 Middletown, Rhode Island

(continued)

1. God uses marriage to symbolize the new relationship between Jesus and ourselves. What are the qualities and responsibilities that marriage brings to mind for you and how can they be applied to your faith?

2. Are there some "old wineskins" in your life (for example, previous experience, knowledge, old prejudices) that you need to change?

3. What are you doing to become more aware of your need for renewal and letting go, so you can keep your wineskins soft, supple and flexible?

—Archdiocese of San Antonio
   St. Anthony of Padua Parish
   San Antonio, Texas

Ninth Sunday of Ordinary Time (B)

Reading I: Deuteronomy 5:12-15
Reading II: 2 Corinthians 4:6-11
Gospel: Mark 2:23—3:6

Scripture Focus

The sabbath rest, which began as a way to rest from labor and enjoy the presence of the Lord, became an overwhelming duty to be observed. In Jesus' day, for example, religious leaders listed thirty-nine specific works people were forbidden to perform. One of these, gathering the crops in the field, rightly forbids heavy field work. But the Pharisees, the religious leaders and teachers, accuse Jesus' followers of violating this rule, even though they're merely plucking and eating stray kernels of grain as they walked. Jesus' point is that rules and regulations in and of themselves shouldn't take precedence over genuine human need. When Jesus also cures the man with the shriveled hand, he makes his point clear: People are more important than rules.

Life Focus

1. Relate a time when your behavior was like the Pharisees: sticking to the "letter of the law" rather than considering the needs of others.

2. Reflect on what the Sabbath means to us. Do we respect the rights of everyone?

3. Relate a time when you felt the law of the Church did not fit a particular situation. How did you react?

4. How do you uphold the observance of the Sabbath with the emphasis today on the seven-day shopping and work week?

—Diocese of Rockhampton
   Callide Valley Parish
   Biloela Q, Australia

Tenth Sunday of Ordinary Time (B)

Reading I: Genesis 3:9-15
Reading II: 2 Corinthians 4:13—5:1
Gospel: Mark 3:20-35

Scripture Focus

In Mark's Gospel the religious leaders mistakenly call
Jesus' power satanic. His relatives think he is crazy.
But we know from the first reading from Genesis that
God has subdued Satan and promised redemption
through his Son. This is what Jesus is getting at in his
story about a household divided. Saving this
household means first subduing the strong man. Jesus
can overpower Satan because his power is God's.
When his family arrives, he explains that accepting
him and doing the will of God is more important than
blood ties.

Life Focus

1. In what way is your own life divided? How can you
make it more whole?

2. Do you take responsibility for your own decisions,
or are you influenced by someone else?

3. Can you describe an occasion when you have
"hidden" from God? Why?

4. What does "doing the will of God" mean in your
everyday life?

—Chase Valley
  Pietermaritzburg, South Africa

1. Share a personal experience where you bowed to
temptation and took full responsibility for your
actions.

2. What must I do to be a follower of Jesus today? What
is expected of me?

3. Since no one has seen God, what draws you to
believe in God?

—Diocese of Corpus Christi
  Sts. Cyril and Methodius Church
  Corpus Christi, Texas

Eleventh Sunday of Ordinary Time (B)

Reading I: Ezekiel 17:22-24
Reading II: 2 Corinthians 5:6-10
Gospel: Mark 4:26-34

Scripture Focus

Jesus often teaches in parables, sayings or stories that compare God's ways to ordinary life. The images get our attention, and the puzzling conclusions keep us thinking about their meaning. If we are open to God, we come to understand. Today's parable speaks about the seed growing on its own. It has the power. The planter does not know how or notice the growth beneath the soil. He can be anxious or fret, but it is not his power that makes the seed grow. The parable of the mustard seed speaks about the very small beginnings of God's Kingdom. God's Kingdom grows from those who heed his words. Most people do not understand about God's Kingdom. But the Lord keeps taking the disciples aside and explaining to them. Those who are willing to follow the Lord and listen to his teachings will come to understand the truth of the Kingdom.

Life Focus

1. Tell a contemporary parable of the reign of God that speaks to people in today's world.

2. In your personal life or your small church community, what small thing has become a big or important thing?

3. What have you done in love and service to help the reign of God?

—St. Jude Thaddeus Small Christian Community
   Musoma, Tanzania

Twelfth Sunday of Ordinary Time (B)

Reading I: Job 38:1, 8-11
Reading II: 2 Corinthians 5:14-17
Gospel: Mark 4:35-41

Scripture Focus

Today's Gospel tells us something about Mark's audience. He was writing to early Christians in Rome who were being persecuted and whose lives were upset and threatened. This situation is represented by the disciples being tossed about by the storm at sea. The Lord is in the boat, but he sleeps. The storm at sea represents the evil that God conquers. In the creation story in Genesis, God commands and brings order and calm. In the same way, Jesus quiets this storm. Jesus spends a lot of time with his disciples. But, they are a long way from understanding who he is—and a long way from trusting him in storms.

Life Focus

1. How does Jesus "calm the storm" in your personal life or small church community?

2. Give an example of how you trusted others in your small church community. How did it affect you?

3. What images of Jesus come from your own culture and grassroots experience?

—St. Jude Thaddeus Small Christian Community
   Musoma, Tanzania

Thirteenth Sunday of Ordinary Time (B)

Reading I: Wisdom 1:13-15, 2:23-24
Reading II: 2 Corinthians 8:7, 9, 13-15
Gospel: Mark 5:21-43

Scripture Focus

The Gospel reading shows Jesus' victory over the forces of evil and death. It also shows two desperate people. A father begs Jesus to help his sick daughter. An afflicted woman reaches out to Jesus for a cure. Both people put aside fears in their frantic search for help. By seeking Jesus, Jairus risks the ridicule of his fellow synagogue officials. The unclean woman risks the crowd's anger, and possibly Jesus' anger as well, for her touch. Jesus responds to both tenderly. He calms their fears, confirms their faith and restores the woman to health and Jairus' daughter to new life. Jesus overpowers sickness and death. He answers people's spoken and unspoken needs. "God formed [humans] to be imperishable," says the author of Wisdom. Each of us must trust God's plan.

Life Focus

1. Relate an experience when someone approached you in faith and asked for help.

2. What are the daily routines that drain you in your faith life?

3. Describe a time when the storms of life seemed much more real than God's presence.

4. Relate an experience when someone affirmed you (built you up) and helped you in your struggle.

—Diocese of London
   Essex County
   Cottam, Ontario, Canada

Fourteenth Sunday of Ordinary Time (B)

Reading I: Ezekiel 2:2-5
Reading II: 2 Corinthians 12:7-10
Gospel: Mark 6:1-6

Scripture Focus

Today's readings give us courage even though they speak of failure and rejection because people resist God's word. Jesus' own family, friends and townspeople turn him off. Jesus returns home. A crowd comes to the synagogue to hear him speak. Jesus appears ordinary, like one of them. But his words are amazing. His own kinspeople and townspeople do not have the faith of his followers. They do not see God's Spirit at work. Jesus, like Ezekiel and Paul, is distressed by the response of those he has sent to save. But their rejection does not stop his mission. Jesus cures the sick and moves on to teach others.

Life Focus

1. When have you felt hurt when trying to do something good for another?

2. Relate an experience in your life when you were acknowledged by another person.

3. What prevents you from believing in the goodness of others—sometimes in your own relatives and friends?

4. What keeps you going when you don't feel support?

—Archdiocese of Toronto
   Epiphany of Our Lord
   Scarboro, Ontario, Canada

Fifteenth Sunday of Ordinary Time (B)

Reading I: Amos 7:12-15
Reading II: Ephesians 1:3-14
Gospel: Mark 6:7-13

Scripture Focus

The Twelve are sent to towns of Galilee. It is a trial mission that looks ahead to the Christian mission to the world at large. All Christians are to speak for God in the world, even when the world does not care to listen. Jesus shares with the Twelve his powers over the forces of evil. Jesus says to get moving on this mission right away. The Twelve are to travel light. If they are offered hospitality, they should accept it. If not, they are to shake the dust from their feet, which is what pious Jews did when they returned from unholy territory. Jesus did not tell the Twelve to preach about God's reign. That task belonged to Jesus. They were to be much like John the Baptizer preparing for Jesus' mission. They were happy with their success.

Life Focus

1. Describe a time in your life when you were genuinely lacking resources, but the task got done in spite of your poverty.

2. Share a time when you were able to let go of the disappointment of your failures and get on with your life.

3. How did you feel when called away on an emergency and you had to leave without any of the usual necessities?

4. Relate a time in your life when your attitude shifted from "No way, I can't do it" to "I certainly can." What caused the shift?

—Diocese of St. Paul
  St. John the Baptist Church
  Fort McMurray, Alberta, Canada

Sixteenth Sunday of Ordinary Time (B)

Reading I: Jeremiah 23:1-6
Reading II: Ephesians 2:13-18
Gospel: Mark 6:30-34

Scripture Focus

Jesus looks at the crowd with great feeling. They have no one to feed them with the teaching that will give them life or with the physical food to stay alive. Jesus appreciates how vulnerable people are and how fragile their lives are. Like sheep, they will die without a shepherd to keep them together, show them the way and feed them. Seeing their need, Jesus himself begins to teach. He becomes shepherd to the leaderless flock. Jesus calls his disciples to be the kind of shepherd he is. The disciples, of course, will not understand this kind of leadership until after the death and resurrection of Jesus.

Life Focus

1. When have you felt let down or disappointed by someone you looked to for leadership, guidance or direction?

2. Where is the "out-of-the-way place" that gives you peace? Why do you feel this way about this place?

3. When have you tried to escape the needs of others only to find that *their needs* for your attention were greater than *your need* to be away from it all? How did you feel about the demands placed on you?

4. When in your life have you felt like a sheep without a shepherd, in need of spiritual and/or physical care? Where or from whom did you seek care?

—Diocese of Baton Rouge
  Holy Rosary Parish
  St. Amant, Louisiana

Seventeenth Sunday of Ordinary Time (B)

Reading I: 2 Kings 4:42-44
Reading II: Ephesians 4:1-6
Gospel: John 6:1-15

Scripture Focus

Both the first reading and the Gospel today tell stories of God feeding hungry people through the words and works of prophets. For the next five Sundays, we will hear the Bread of Life teaching from John's Gospel. For John, all of Jesus' acts are "signs"—sacraments—that point to a deeper reality. It is clear that the people do not appreciate the deeper meaning of the miracle of the multiplication of the loaves. The reaction of the crowd showed that they thought wrongly that Jesus was the triumphant and political Messiah. So Jesus goes "back to the mountains alone." The people had indeed misread the sign.

Life Focus

1. Relate a time when you were so engrossed in something important that you forgot to eat.

2. Describe a time when you were surprised that your limited resources were sufficient.

3. Relate a time when your prayers were answered on God's terms rather than your own.

—Diocese of Spokane
  St. Mary Parish
  Spokane, Washington

1. Share an experience in the recent past in which you recognized a definite sign of the Lord working in your life.

2. Describe a time when you experienced abundance in your life.

3. When have you shared your small amount with another? How did this make a difference in the person's life and/or in yours?

4. Relate a time in your life when you were refreshed by someone.

5. From your experience, when did you get so caught up in the physical needs—just making a living—that there was no time and energy for anything else?

—Diocese of Las Cruces
  Immaculate Heart of Mary Cathedral
  Las Cruces, New Mexico

Eighteenth Sunday of Ordinary Time (B)

Reading I: Exodus 16:2-4, 12-15
Reading II: Ephesians 4:17, 20-24
Gospel: John 6:24-35

Scripture Focus

Jesus had just fed the Israelites of his day with "bread from heaven," but they saw only the "bread." They followed him back across the lake to Capernaum. They were hoping for more free food. Jesus uses their question to try to teach them the deeper meaning of the "bread from heaven." He reproaches them for being so concerned about food. They have missed the meaning of the feeding. They do not see this as a "sign" pointing to a deeper reality. When they ask what they must *do* to perform works pleasing to God, Jesus says, in effect, "nothing." They are asked simply to accept him as the one God has sent. This faith is a free gift of God. The mention of faith makes them impatient. They want action. The crowd is operating on the material level. They are hoping for an endless supply of food. Jesus startles them by saying he is bread which gives life. They must believe in him. He will satisfy them forever.

Life Focus

1. In a society that offers instant gratification and the pursuit of comfort and convenience, what can you do to keep your focus on Jesus?

2. Where have you seen Jesus this past week in your life? What message did he have for you, and how did you respond?

3. What are some things you take for granted? Share an experience when you've taken life's pleasures for granted and your expectations weren't life's reality. How did you cope?

4. Most families bring their problems to the dinner table. When have you brought your problems to the Lord's table?

5. How has your attitude toward material things changed over your lifetime? Name an experience that shows this change.

—Archdiocese of San Antonio
  St. Francis of Assisi Catholic Community
  Laughlin Air Force Base, Texas

Nineteenth Sunday of Ordinary Time (B)

Reading I: 1 Kings 19:4-8
Reading II: Ephesians 4:30—5:2
Gospel: John 6:41-51

Scripture Focus

The theme of "bread from heaven" is developed in many ways in this chapter of John's Gospel. Today's reading opens with the people murmuring. Since he was born in time, since the people knew his father and his mother, Jesus simply could not have come from heaven. Jesus does not meet their objection directly. He raises the discussion to a higher level. To understand him it is necessary to have faith. Only God can give faith. God holds out the gift to all who are open to receive it. Faith is acceptance of Jesus, and this faith in Jesus, eating the living bread, gives eternal life.

Life Focus

1. Relate an experience when you had a difficult time seeing Christ in someone you know well.

2. Describe a time when you felt empty inside. What helped you through that empty period?

3. Describe a time when you offered help to another and were rejected. How did you feel, and what did you do?

4. How does believing in eternal life affect your daily living?

—Archdiocese of Atlanta
   St. Thomas Aquinas Church
   Alpharetta, Georgia

1. Where does your life need nourishing?

2. Relate an experience when you surprised yourself by doing something you ordinarily would be unable to do.

3. Describe a time when someone fulfilled a hunger or a need in your life.

4. Relate a time when you were misjudged or misinterpreted when you told the truth or did something good.

—Diocese of Grand Island
   North Platte, Nebraska

Twentieth Sunday of Ordinary Time (B)

Reading I: Proverbs 9:1-6
Reading II: Ephesians 5:15-20
Gospel: John 6:51-58

Scripture Focus

John's Gospel has no direct account of the institution of the Eucharist at the Last Supper. Rather, it includes this sermon on the Bread of Life that we have been hearing for the past several weeks. The statement of the opening verse, "the *bread* that I will give is my flesh for the life of the world," is very close to the account in Luke's Gospel of Jesus blessing bread at the Last Supper and saying "This is my body given for you." Accepting the teaching of Jesus, the Liturgy of the Word, important as this is, only prepares us to share his body and blood. Participation in the Eucharist brings present possession of "eternal life" and is thus a pledge of eventual resurrection.

Life Focus

1. Jesus puts great emphasis on the "flesh and blood" reality of the food we now call the Eucharist. Name other ways you "feed on" the "flesh and blood" reality of Jesus.

2. What have you done with this "life" received in the Eucharist?

—Santiago, Chile

1. Describe an experience when you have been the "bread of life" for others.

—Diocese of Grand Island
   North Platte, Nebraska

Twenty-First Sunday of Ordinary Time (B)

Reading I: Joshua 24:1-2, 15-17, 18
Reading II: Ephesians 5:21-32
Gospel: John 6:60-69

Scripture Focus

Faced with Jesus' claim to be the real bread from heaven, the truth, the revelation of the Father, his disciples had to make a decision. Today's Gospel reading gives their reaction to that claim. Many reject his words and refuse to believe that he "came down" from heaven. Jesus told them to "stop murmuring" and pointed out the need for that faith which only God can give. The Twelve remain with Jesus. They were the ones who would "remain with Jesus" once he ascended to the Father. Peter sums up their faith, accepting the revelation of Jesus with the words, "Lord, to whom shall we go? You have the words of eternal life." The people who deserted him wanted answers they could understand. Their faith was weak. The apostles did not understand either, but because they loved Jesus, they believed and accepted without understanding. We, too, cannot really understand how Jesus is present in the Eucharist. We cannot know, intellectually, how bread and wine became his "body and blood." When we make our act of faith, however, we become one with him in a special, life-giving way.

Life Focus

1. Describe how your experience of the Eucharist has changed over the course of your life and how this has affected you.

2. Describe a struggle you had which led to a deeper faith.

3. Relate an experience that has shaken your faith.

4. Describe an experience when you have taken a risk without fully understanding the outcome. What effect did it have on your life?

—Diocese of Cleveland
   Our Lady Help of Christians
   Litchfield, Ohio

Twenty-Second Sunday of Ordinary Time (B)

Reading I: Deuteronomy 4:1-2, 6-8
Reading II: James 1:17-18, 21-22, 27
Gospel: Mark 7:1-8, 14-15, 21-23

Scripture Focus

Jesus' words are strong about getting caught up in what one does on the outside. Religion cannot be all externals. Jesus takes the offensive here. He adapts a quote from Isaiah about paying lip service to God with no heart. He warns them about insisting that human rules are God's will. In fact, the Book of Deuteronomy clearly says that nothing may be added or taken away from God's law. Deuteronomy speaks of God's law as a way to show gratitude for God's great love. God chose and formed people freely. These laws of God are not a heavy burden nor a way to win God's love; they are simply a way to respond with love to God's goodness. The Pharisees took God's law seriously and followed it with devotion. But a few Pharisees forgot the heart of religion—God's relationship with people—and got trapped in mere regulations. This passage can speak to our own lives in the Church today.

Life Focus

1. Describe a time when your heart led you to do something good, but the "law" stood in the way.

2. Name an experience when "the way we (your Church, society, your small church community, your personal life) do things" got in the way of what's really important.

3. Relate a time when you judged a person unacceptable because of externals.

—Diocese of Monterey
 Monterey, California

Twenty-Third Sunday of Ordinary Time (B)

Reading I: Isaiah 35:4-7
Reading II: James 2:1-5
Gospel: Mark 7:31-37

Scripture Focus

The cure of the deaf-mute in today's Gospel points to a deeper reality. We are told that Jesus returned "into the district of the ten cities." This was Gentile country. The deaf-mute symbolizes the Gentiles who had to have their ears opened to God's word before they could proclaim it. For Mark's community, which was mostly Gentile, the man's cure dramatized their hearing the Good News. God draws near to all, Jews and Gentiles alike.

Life Focus

1. Describe a situation in your life when a gentle touch brought peace.

2. Describe an experience when you were accepted or helped by a stranger. How did this experience make you feel?

3. Recall an experience when you reached out to someone beyond your circle of friends.

4. What do you need in order to hear life better?

5. Who are the people in society or in the church that you have trouble hearing?

—Archdiocese of New Orleans
 St. Peter Parish
 Covington, Louisiana

Twenty-Fourth Sunday of Ordinary Time (B)

Reading I: Isaiah 50:4-9
Reading II: James 2:14-18
Gospel: Mark 8:27-35

Scripture Focus

Today's Gospel is a key passage in Mark, a sort of hinge between the first and second parts of his Gospel. The first part is all about reactions to Jesus, looking forward to his final rejection in Jerusalem. In today's passage, we get the reaction of his own disciples, a crucial reaction. Peter, who appears to speak for all the disciples, gives a clear and direct reply. Jesus is the Messiah. But Jesus suspects that Peter's idea of a messiah is off the mark. Jesus predicts the Passion that will be the backbone of the next section. The emphasis will now be on the suffering Son of Man. Peter's idea of a popular political messiah gets a public reprimand from Jesus. This leads to the first of three instructions on discipleship. All share the fact that following Jesus will mean suffering with him through a life of selfless love.

Life Focus

1. Describe an experience when you were willing to pay a price to follow the Lord.

2. Relate an experience that led you to a change of heart.

3. Tell of a time when you or someone you know felt alienated from the Church. How did that affect you?

4. What kind of action do you take when someone in your parish appears to be rejected?

—Archdiocese of Denver
Denver, Colorado

Twenty-Fifth Sunday of Ordinary Time (B)

Reading I: Wisdom 2:12, 17-20
Reading II: James 3:16—4:3
Gospel: Mark 9:30-37

Scripture Focus

After the second prediction of suffering, the disciples fail or refuse to ask about its meaning. Instead, they do the exact opposite of Jesus' teaching: They struggle with each other for position and power. Jesus answers with a symbolic action that is stronger than words. He embraces a child, a symbol of powerlessness. He directs them not to build up a power structure but to embrace powerlessness. In the same way, the power of the Christian community will be in powerlessness.

Life Focus

1. Describe an experience when you gained insight from an experience of being defenseless and powerless.

2. Why is it difficult for you to be last of all? Why is it worth it?

3. Tell of a time when your life was enriched by a person who gave up power willingly.

4. Relate a situation when you were tempted to try to control another's life or situation.

—Archdiocese of Washington
Washington, D.C.

Twenty-Sixth Sunday of Ordinary Time (B)

Reading I: Numbers 11:25-29
Reading II: James 5:1-6
Gospel: Mark 9:38-43, 45, 47-48

Scripture Focus

There is always a temptation in Church communities to control and possess all the ways God works and not give credit to anyone who is not of our kind. In today's Gospel the apostles forbid a man from casting out demons because he is not in their group of followers of Jesus. The same narrowness shows up in the first reading. Joshua complains that two Israelites are speaking for God with the power of God's spirit. They were not part of the seventy helpers at the special ceremony. Moses answers much like Jesus. The disciples are told they belong to Christ. The phrase is literally, "in the name of Christ." This name is powerful enough, not only to cast out demons, but to gather people into the person of Christ. Anything done for those who belong to Christ will be appreciated by God. Anything done to hurt or stand in the way of one who belongs to Christ deserves punishment. Any sacrifice is worth the effort to belong to Christ.

Life Focus

1. Describe an experience in which a person was misjudged because he or she was not "one of us."

2. Relate an experience when God's power or love came to you through an unlikely person.

3. Name a time when your action became an obstacle to God's power working.

4. What do you need to cut out in order to be more fully alive?

—Diocese of Cleveland
    Lorain, Ohio

Twenty-Seventh Sunday of Ordinary Time (B)

Reading I: Genesis 2:18-24
Reading II: Hebrews 2:9-11
Gospel: Mark 10:2-16

Scripture Focus

In Mark's Gospel Jesus goes beyond the Law of Moses and back to God's own command. Jesus teaches the clear ideal of Genesis 2. The Hebrews saw a human person as body, soul and spirit—all together. You are your body. So, when a man and woman "become one body," they are like one person. There is no domination of man over woman here. Man and woman complement one another, complete each other.

Life Focus

1. Describe an experience in your life when, because of your trust in a person, you accepted something difficult to understand.

2. How have you lived through the experience of not being accepted by an individual or group?

3. Relate an experience in your marriage or in a close relationship when you felt alone or felt a strong sense of belonging.

4. How has a married couple contributed to your life?

5. How have you helped heal the hurt of someone who has divorced?

—Archdiocese of Hartford
    Hartford, Connecticut

Twenty-Eighth Sunday of Ordinary Time (B)

Reading I: Wisdom 7:7-11
Reading II: Hebrews 4:12-13
Gospel: Mark 10:17-30

Scripture Focus

Today's Gospel illustrates the frequent conflict between wisdom and wealth. The man who asked the secret of everlasting life was clearly a thoroughly good person. But Jesus senses in this man an attitude of not needing anyone else. Jesus tells him, in effect, "All the resources on which you rely are useless. Get rid of them, trust in God, and follow me." The challenge here was not to *poverty* as such, but to trust. Salvation is God's gift, not a reward for human efforts.

Life Focus

1. Relate an experience when you had to rely on someone other than yourself. How did this make you feel?

2. When have you abandoned something or someone you valued in order to better follow the gospel?

3. When have you worked too hard to earn respect or love?

4. What would you let go of right now to increase your trust in God?

—Diocese of Metuchen
  Metuchen, New Jersey

Twenty-Ninth Sunday of Ordinary Time (B)

Reading I: Isaiah 53:10-11
Reading II: Hebrews 4:14-16
Gospel: Mark 10:35-45

Scripture Focus

Today Jesus predicts his suffering, rejection and resurrection for the third time. The pattern is always the same: Jesus predicts his suffering; the disciples fail to understand; Jesus then teaches clearly about himself and about what following him means. In his third prediction of suffering, Jesus describes how he will be handed over to his own people's religious leaders and to the Gentiles and will be spit upon and mocked. James and John, Jesus' inner circle of followers, get caught on the glory promised. They argue for first place. But Jesus points out to them that true greatness is serving the real needs of others—not what the masses of people or the ones in power want. Jesus is that obedient servant of God.

Life Focus

1. Speak of a time when you took the rap for someone else or when someone took the rap for you.

2. When has suffering in your life caused you to see things differently?

3. Describe an experience when you were required to do something you didn't want to do.

—Diocese of Providence
  Providence, Rhode Island

(continued)

1. What effect does this reading have on your pursuit of prominence in your community?

2. Can you recall a personal incident when your prayerful request was seemingly refused, but in hindsight you understood that God answered it?

3. Tell of a time when you were asked what you wanted and then were refused. How did you feel? What did you do?

—Archdiocese of San Francisco
    Most Holy Redeemer Parish
    San Francisco, California

Thirtieth Sunday of Ordinary Time (B)

Reading I: Jeremiah 31:7-9
Reading II: Hebrews 5:1-6
Gospel: Mark 10:46-52

Scripture Focus

The second half of Mark's Gospel is all about seeing and not seeing Jesus for who he really is. Three times Jesus predicts his rejection and execution by the leaders. He and the disciples are on the long journey to Jerusalem where he will be seen clearly. The disciples refuse to see. They cannot and will not recognize such a leader. Bartimaeus, even in his blindness, sees and shouts to Jesus as the Son of David, a title for the messiah. When Jesus asks, the blind man is simple and clear and he follows Jesus on the road to Jerusalem—to suffering, dying and rising. Bartimaeus calls Jesus "Master." Bartimaeus is the new disciple going along with Jesus.

Life Focus

1. What do you need to see in order to follow God better in your life?

2. Recall an experience when your values were questioned and you either shouted louder or shut up.

3. Describe a time when you were moved to change your way of seeing things because of a very important person in your life.

4. When have you acted on blind faith?

—Archdiocese of St. Louis
    St. Louis, Missouri

(continued)

1. Relate a time when you found Christ approachable.

2. Give an example of a time in your life when you called out for Christ's help and you found him available.

3. Think of a time when Christ might have said to you, "Your faith has made you well."

—Archdiocese of San Francisco
 Most Holy Redeemer Parish
 San Francisco, California

Thirty-First Sunday of Ordinary Time (B)

Reading I: Deuteronomy 6:2-6
Reading II: Hebrews 7:23-28
Gospel: Mark 12:28-34

Scripture Focus

Today's Gospel is part of a series of six conflict stories that take place in Jerusalem during the last week of Jesus' life. Jerusalem will reject Jesus. In the midst of this controversy, the leaders are already plotting to kill him. And yet in a surprising twist, this scribe is honest in asking about the most important way of following God. Jesus answers as any good Jewish leader would with the two great commandments. He links them together. Whether Jewish teachers of the time did the same linking together or whether this is original with Jesus, we do not know. But the link is clear. Loving self, neighbor and God go together. One cannot love God without developing a reverence for God's children. The scribe goes much further than a good and devout Jew of the time would go. He says that this double law of love is more important than temple worship. Jesus tells him he is not far from the reign of God.

Life Focus

1. Speak of a surprising way someone touched you with concern recently.

2. What keeps you from noticing love present in your life?

3. Who of the three—you, others, God—is the most difficult for you to have real regard for? Why?

4. When did you feel God was asking too much of you in loving your neighbor?

—Archdiocese of Santa Fe
 Santa Fe, New Mexico

Thirty-Second Sunday of Ordinary Time (B)

Reading I: 1 Kings 17:10-16
Reading II: Hebrews 9:24-28
Gospel: Mark 12:38-44

Scripture Focus

Today's reading from Kings illustrates several things: God's care for the poor, even the foreign poor (Zarephath was over Israel's border in what is now Lebanon); Elijah's activity as his agent; and, in the context of today's liturgy, the trusting generosity of a widow who sacrifices her own livelihood to the needs of another. Quite clearly we are invited to connect her to the widow of the Gospel reading. In Mark's Gospel the poor widow who contributed "all that she had to live on" is sharply contrasted with the wealthy who gave sizable amounts from their surplus wealth. The rich do not depend on God. They have plenty to live on. The widow now has only God and God's people to lean upon.

Life Focus

1. When have you "paraded" in your robes, accepted respect in public and in places of honor, but disregarded the needs of others?

2. In those areas where we are "wealthy," it is easy to share with others. Share some moments when you gave to others even when you felt poor and giving was a big risk.

3. How have others helped you discover what is important in loving God?

—Santiago, Chile

1. By giving from her "want," the widow shows her trust in God. Can you recall an experience when you let go and put your trust in God?

2. The scribes say long prayers and Jesus disapproves. How would you describe your prayer life and its development?

3. From your experience, what are some practical ways you can contribute to the Church besides money?

4. The widow in Israel's history stands for someone who has no support and is helpless. In what practical ways have you helped the helpless and disadvantaged in your community?

5. Jesus criticizes the scribes for being religious in the wrong way. What are the qualities you find in a person you consider to be religious?

6. From your experience, describe a time in your life when you believed that God was calling you to give from your want.

—Archdiocese of Philadelphia
St. Andrew Parish
Newtown, Pennsylvania

Thirty-Third Sunday of Ordinary Time (B)

Reading I: Daniel 12:1-3
Reading II: Hebrews 10:11-14, 18
Gospel: Mark 13:24-32

Scripture Focus

As the Church year nears its end, the readings also speak of the end time. These readings were written during times of trial and persecution, and their purpose is to encourage people not to give up. Today's reading from Daniel comes just one hundred sixty-five years before Jesus. It speaks of great conflict—even the earth will shake and the stars will fall—but for the first time in the Old Testament, there is a very clear belief in the resurrection of the faithful and punishment for evil. God's kingdom will win over every kind of evil. God's faithful who do good and lead others to goodness (justice) will shine with God's own light. The Gospel proclaims that Jesus will come at the end of time to call his people from all over the world to share in his victory. All the physical world—earth, sun, moon, stars—will be under and belong to him.

Life Focus

1. In tough times, what keeps you going?

2. If the world were ending tomorrow, how would you experience today differently? What would you do differently today?

3. In what way do you need to persevere right now?

—Archdiocese of Hartford
 Hartford, Connecticut

Solemnity of Christ the King (B)

Reading I: Daniel 7:13-14
Reading II: Revelation 1:5-8
Gospel: John 18:33-37

Scripture Focus

Today's Gospel is all about the world not recognizing Jesus. Neither the Roman world nor the Jewish religious community recognized who Jesus really was. They call Jesus "king," but they do not realize the truth of what they say. In John's Gospel Jesus is in control of the situation. He is already the victor. He walks the way of the cross like a king to his throne and he rules from the cross. Jesus' power is the truth he has and the truth he is. His kingdom is not of this world, but his kingdom is very much coming into this world of ours. That kingdom calls into question the way things are done by the rulers of this world.

Life Focus

1. How have you recently experienced the conflict between the values of the kingdom and the values that modern society preaches?

2. Relate a personal experience of being rejected as Christ was.

3. Jesus testified to the truth. When have you been challenged to do the same?

4. What are the obstacles that pull you away from following Jesus?

—Diocese of Hamilton
 Hamilton, Ontario, Canada

Commentaries and Questions for Cycle C

First Sunday of Advent (C)

Reading I: Jeremiah 33:14-16
Reading II: 1 Thessalonians 3:12—4:2
Gospel: Luke 21:25-28, 34-36

Scripture Focus

During Advent we remember Jesus' coming at the first Christmas and we are getting ready for this year's Christmas. But, Jesus' first coming really looks forward to his final coming at the end. The early Christians thought this second coming would happen during their lifetime. The Gospel writers wanted to make it clear that Jesus never promised this. But, Luke wants his Church community and ours to wait with expectation and hope. His Gospel begins with God's message to key people not to be afraid. At the predictions of the end of the world, Jesus again encourages people not to be afraid. The Son of Man will come to transform the world.

Life Focus

1. In the hustle and bustle of everyday life, what are the situations and events that scare you?

2. Who or what gave you the courage to go on when things seemed to be falling apart?

3. Describe an experience when hope has carried you through a trying time.

4. We all have to wait for different things. What has the experience of waiting been like for you during different times of your life?

5. What has to change in this world of ours for God's rule to come?

—Archdiocese of St. Boniface
  Manitoba, Canada

Second Sunday of Advent (C)

Reading I: Baruch 5:1-9
Reading II: Philippians 1:4-6, 8-11
Gospel: Luke 3:1-6

Scripture Focus

The First Sunday of Advent looks to the final coming of Jesus in glory at the end of time. The second and third Advent Sundays look to Jesus' first coming and feature John the Baptist as the first to announce Jesus' ministry. Luke introduces John with a list of all the political and religious leaders of the time. All these leaders hold power and will reject Jesus, but God's call is greater than any opposition. John's message speaks to us as much as it did to the people of his time: Make a straight way for the one who is to come. Change your life and your attitude. Repent. Make room!

Life Focus

1. John the Baptist's message is for all times. In what areas are you challenged to change in the midst of all the worldly attitudes around you?

2. How are you called to live the Good News concretely in your local communities—family, neighborhood, small church community?

3. John the Baptist prepared the way for Jesus. How do you announce the coming of the Lord?

—St. Peter Claver Church
  Nairobi, Kenya

Third Sunday of Advent (C)

Reading I: Zephaniah 3:14-18
Reading II: Philippians 4:4-7
Gospel: Luke 3:10-18

Scripture Focus

John the Baptizer was looking forward to and preparing for the coming of a great prophet, which was to signal the dawn of God's reign. His message was a stern, no-nonsense one: Repent or be damned! He also gives people specific examples of how they are to repent. People who have more than they need are to share with those who do not have enough. Tax collectors must stop cheating people. Soldiers and heads of state must stop intimidating people. The people who heard John wondered if he were the coming Messiah, but he quickly points to one "far superior to himself." The difference is indicated by their baptisms—one with water, one with the fire of the Holy Spirit.

Life Focus

1. If you were to ask John the Baptist this same question today, "What am I to do then?" how would he answer you?

2. In our personal lives, how can we imitate John the Baptist as we proclaim the Good News?

3. How can we radiate to others the joy of God's presence within us?

—Guajiquiro
   La Paz, Honduras

1. Describe a time when you believe God lifted a burden from you and "renew(ed) you in his love."

2. Relate a time in your life when you felt discouraged, and it seemed there was little reason for celebration. What restored your hope?

3. How does anxiety prevent you from accepting God's peace? For this week, how could you "dismiss (some) anxiety from your mind"?

4. Describe a time when it seemed to you that God had a part in making a bad situation into a good one. How has this change affected your life?

5. "Everyone should see how unselfish you are." Who will experience your unselfishness this week?

6. "The people were full of anticipation...." How will you foster in yourself and others a greater sense of anticipation for the celebration of Christ's birth?

—Diocese of Peoria
   St. Francis of Assisi Newman Center
   Western Illinois University
   Macomb, Illinois

Fourth Sunday of Advent (C)

Reading I: Micah 5:1-4
Reading II: Hebrews 10:5-10
Gospel: Luke 1:39-45

Scripture Focus

Luke's account of the visitation is a lovely human story. In addition, there are deep statements about God and the desired relationship with God. The account reveals profound faith in the Lordship of Jesus and the power of the Holy Spirit. Mary is blessed because of her trusting acceptance of God's plan for her. She is the model disciple, a model for all. She hears the word of God and keeps it, not really knowing what lies in store for her. Also, Mary's blessedness comes from the "fruit of her womb." Elizabeth voices the fundamental Christian faith in the Lordship of Jesus: "But who am I that the mother of my Lord should come to me?"

Life Focus

1. Share a time in your life when you've been asked to believe in God's promise when all circumstances would have you believe otherwise.

2. State when in your life you've been filled with enthusiasm and joy and proclaimed Jesus as Lord.

3. Compare a time you said "yes" to God, when you "went out in haste," to a time you went out with careful deliberation.

4. Relate an incident in your life when you were aware of the Holy Spirit working in someone else.

5. In what circumstances do you find it most difficult to be honest and open about what you think and feel?

—Diocese of Richmond
  Parish of the Holy Spirit
  Virginia Beach, Virginia

Solemnity of Christmas

(See Cycle A, page 7.)

Feast of the Holy Family (C)

Reading I: Sirach 3:2-6, 12-14
Reading II: Colossians 3:12-21
Gospel: Luke 2:41-52

Scripture Focus

Children always love to hear stories about when they were little. They never tire of hearing the same ones again and again. As adults, we hear these same stories with a different perspective. In them we see a glimpse of what has made us who we are. In the same way, Luke uses stories of Jesus' early years to prepare us for his ministry. In the temple, his "Father's house," Jesus is at home. For now, he belongs to his parents, but that is not where he really belongs. We have seen a glimpse of the future. As Jesus "had to be" in his "Father's house," so must we make our own homes our "Father's house" by honoring one another. In Christ, we see *our* true identity as God's children, God's "chosen ones," God's family in grace.

Life Focus

1. What do you think were the feelings Jesus' parents had during the three days they were searching for him? Share a time when you may have had similar feelings about a lost child or a loved one.

2. Describe a time in your life when you had to let go of a person or a project that had become dear to you. How was your belief in the power of Jesus involved in this letting go?

3. Every family is a "holy family." In your family situation, what can you do to better recognize the holiness in each member?

—Archdiocese of Indianapolis
  Office of Catholic Education
  Indianapolis, Indiana

Feast of Epiphany

(See Cycle A, page 10.)

Baptism of the Lord (C)

Reading I: Isaiah 42:1-4, 6-7
Reading II: Acts 10:34-38
Gospel: Luke 3:15-16, 21-22

Scripture Focus

Luke tells us that John prepares the way for Jesus' ministry by the baptism he preaches. That baptism not only marks the beginning of Christ's ministry, but it also marks the dawn of a new era in human history. Our eyes are drawn from one figure to another: In John we see the promise; in Jesus, the fulfillment. As Luke records events, John will soon fade out of the picture entirely. He is "water" compared to "fire." He is herald compared to the One he proclaimed. He preached a promise. It would come true. As John prepared the way for the Lord, so must we in our own lives. As we were given a new birth in the Holy Spirit with our own Baptism, we must hear and obey God's word in our lives every day.

Life Focus

1. John the Baptist prepared the way for the Lord. How do you "prepare the way for the Lord" in your own life and in the lives of others?

2. Baptism prepared Jesus for his mission and life's work. What has your Baptism asked you to do? How have you responded?

—Archdiocese of Atlanta
   St. Thomas Aquinas Church
   Alpharetta, Georgia

1. Describe a time when you noticed a real renewing of life, either in yourself, in others or in society. What was the effect?

—Archdiocese of Los Angeles
   Our Lady of Assumption Church
   Ventura, California

1. Give an example of a time you were reluctant to do as Jesus asked.

—St. Peter Claver Church
   Kingston, Jamaica

1. Describe a time in your life when someone helped you reach your potential.

2. Describe a time when you experienced a new beginning.

—Archdiocese of Cincinnati
   St. Francis of Assisi Parish
   Centerville, Ohio

First Sunday of Lent (C)

Reading I: Deuteronomy 26:4-10
Reading II: Romans 10:8-13
Gospel: Luke 4:1-13

Scripture Focus

The temptation of Jesus in the desert, as told by Luke, was not the first time Jesus was tempted, nor would it be the last. But Luke, like Matthew, uses these three temptations in a powerful way to depict the frequent experiences of Jesus. He struggled with the difficult possibilities open to him in carrying out his mission right up to the agony in the garden. As a human being he was always free to choose his path. But Jesus was also conscious of his loyalty and relationship with God. Nothing will deter Jesus from establishing the Kingdom of God. His deepest trust is to follow God's plan and to carry out his mission according to that plan and none other. Jesus rejects Satan and places his trust in the guidance of God, no matter where that might lead.

Life Focus

1. Describe a time in your life when you asked for proof of God's care for you.

2. Recall an incident when you chose to accept or get out of an everyday hardship in your life.

3. Tell of a time when a temptation revealed something to you about God or yourself.

4. Relate an experience from your life when you wondered whether God cared for you or not.

5. What besides "bread" satisfies the hungers in your life?

—Archdiocese of Cincinnati
   Precious Blood Church
   Dayton, Ohio

Second Sunday of Lent (C)

Reading I: Genesis 15:5-12, 17-18
Reading II: Philippians 3:17—4:1
Gospel: Luke 9:28-36

Scripture Focus

One of the key themes in Luke's Gospel is glory. As Jesus is transfigured, Moses and Elijah appear "in glory." When the apostles awake, they see only Jesus' "glory." Moses and Elijah reveal that Christ's passage would be through suffering to glory. The voice of God identifies Jesus as God's chosen son, and commands the apostles to listen, to listen to what Jesus has just announced—his approaching death and resurrection. In this passage, the glory of God will be revealed.

Life Focus

1. Relate an experience of having to do something difficult or unpleasant that helped another person.

2. Describe a time when you stopped to listen closely to another person.

3. Relate an event that enabled you to carry on through a difficult time in your life.

4. What are some "mountaintop" experiences in your life?

5. What experience these past two weeks helped you see God working in your life?

6. Describe a hardship you experienced that made you a better person.

—Archdiocese of Vancouver
   St. Joseph the Worker Parish
   Richmond, British Columbia, Canada

(continued)

1. Share an experience in your life that you wanted to last forever, that you wished would never end.

2. Tell of a time when you were frustrated trying to share an intense experience with others.

3. Share when you felt fear at being asked to do something difficult.

—County Sligo
  Ireland

Third Sunday of Lent (C)

Reading I: Exodus 3:1-8, 13-15
Reading II: 1 Corinthians 10:1-6, 10-12
Gospel: Luke 13:1-9

Scripture Focus

The fig tree in the parable in today's Gospel represents Jerusalem. Jerusalem was the center of God's chosen people. He loved and cared, cultivated and fertilized. It is time for Jerusalem to bear fruit, but Jerusalem failed. The coming of Jesus as the "sign" of God's love for people can be seen as an extra time of grace given to Jerusalem. But by the time the Gospel was written, Luke's audience would know that Jerusalem had been destroyed. The parable also carries a caution for us: Unless we reform, we too will perish, just as Jerusalem did.

Life Focus

1. Tell how God's calling caused you to look inward and make positive change in your life.

2. You have been asked to speak to a group of teenagers. What experience would you share about how you examine your relationship with God, spouse, friends, colleagues, etc.?

3. Throughout our lives we are faced with situations like the man with the fig tree. When were you recently faced with a challenging situation that required your patience and nurturing? How did your faith see you through?

4. What are some "fruits" you need to cultivate more carefully in your life? What is keeping you from being productive?

—Archdiocese of Denver
  Light of the World Catholic Parish
  Littleton, Colorado

Fourth Sunday of Lent (C)

Reading I: Joshua 5:9, 10-12
Reading II: 2 Corinthians 5:17-21
Gospel: Luke 15:1-3, 11-32

Scripture Focus

The parable of the prodigal son is one of the best known of all the stories Jesus told. The parable is about divine mercy and the desire "to return to the father." Luke has in mind tax collectors and sinners who were "drawing near" to Jesus. The group of Pharisees and scribes, represented by the elder son, only complain and criticize. According to the way they see it, they have served God and obeyed the Law. They don't understand how sinners can also be sons and daughters of God. For Luke, the religious leaders who keep all the rules and think they can earn salvation by their own efforts are farther away from God than the sinners.

Life Focus

1. Which of these two sons is more like you? Reflect on an experience from your life that would show this.

2. Was there a time when you were away from God? How did you find your way back? What brought you back? How did you feel?

3. How do you handle resentment in your own life experience? What words of advice to deal with resentment could you offer the older brother?

4. The father shows loving patience. Speak of an experience from your life when you had to wait patiently. How did that make you feel?

5. Describe a situation in your life when you found it difficult to ask for forgiveness.

6. Who would you have a difficult time letting back into the Church or the family? Why?

—Diocese of Worcester
  Office of Religious Education
  Worcester, Massachusetts

Fifth Sunday of Lent (C)

Reading I: Isaiah 43:16-21
Reading II: Philippians 3:8-14
Gospel: John 8:1-11

Scripture Focus

The Gospel story of the woman caught in adultery shows Jesus' concern for women put down and exploited. Those who accused the woman were using her to trap Jesus. If he says to let the woman go, he has no regard for the law that says she should be stoned to death. If he agrees that she should be stoned, he goes against his own gospel of compassion. Jesus says nothing; he stoops and scribbles in the sand. He says, "Let the one among you who is without sin be the first to throw a stone at her." The crowd, understandably, drifts away. Jesus is left alone with the woman. He treats her as a real person, with respect. He refuses to condemn her. He tells her to go, but from now on, to avoid this sin.

Life Focus

1. Imagine this scene happening in your life. Who are you in this picture? How is Jesus guiding you toward forgiveness and compassion?

2. In what way does having your sinfulness or faults exposed help you toward greater compassion?

3. Recall a time when your mistakes were not held against you.

4. What do you do to keep from judging others as less than yourself?

5. Tell about a time when your first impression of someone was wrong.

—Archdiocese of San Francisco
  Most Holy Redeemer Parish
  San Francisco, California

Passion/Palm Sunday (C)

Reading I: Isaiah 50:4-7
Reading II: Philippians 2:6-11
Gospel: Luke 22:14—23:56

Scripture Focus

The Passion narrative in Luke's Gospel pulls together many of Jesus' teachings. The Last Supper recalls the meals Jesus shared with outcasts and sinners. Jesus uses this meal and the cross as the entry to the fullness of the heavenly banquet where we will eat again with him and with each other. On the way to Calvary, he continues to call the people to repent, to change their hearts. Jesus continues to reach out and forgive, even from the cross. He forgives his killers and offers salvation to the repentant thief. Jesus dies as he lives, the obedient and faithful servant of God. Because of this he is raised up in the kingdom.

Life Focus

1. What crosses do you carry in your everyday life—sickness, AIDS, marriage conflicts, backbiting and jealousy in personal relationships, civil and tribal wars, etc.?

2. How do you deny Jesus in your everyday life?

3. Jesus suffered when he was innocent. What does this say to you?

—St. Jude Thaddeus Small Christian Community
　Musoma, Tanzania

1. How could you be Christ-like in your daily persecutions?

2. In what way do the people who make you unhappy affect your being a Christian?

3. How do you see God or not see God in your trials and difficulties?

—Blessed Sacrament Congregation
　Assumption Parish
　Davao City, Philippines

Triduum

(See Cycle A, page 18.)

Easter Sunday

(See Cycle A, page 22.)

Second Sunday of Easter (C)

Reading I: Acts 5:12-16
Reading II: Revelation 1:9-11, 12-13, 17-19
Gospel: John 20:19-31

Scripture Focus

The appearance of Jesus that we hear about in today's Gospel involves more than a lack of understanding; it is a definite refusal to understand. Jesus agrees to Thomas' wishes concerning the wounds in his "hands" and "sides." He commands Thomas to "touch" them. But sight is sufficient, and Thomas puts aside his demands. He hears only the final "command" of the Risen Jesus, to replace his unbelief with belief. John turns to those who "have not seen but who have believed." The things "written in this book" challenge those who never saw Jesus to believe.

Life Focus

1. Thomas stands for all believers with reservations. Recall an experience that shows Thomas in you.

2. Jesus' peace is a source of spirit, forgiveness and faith. When did you last pray for forgiveness?

3. Describe a time in your life when it was difficult to feel the presence of Jesus in a time of need.

4. Share an experience of reconciliation.

5. Describe a time when you became convinced that Jesus was real.

—Diocese of Providence
　St. Jude Parish
　Lincoln, Rhode Island

Third Sunday of Easter (C)

Reading I: Acts 5:27-32, 40-41
Reading II: Revelation 5:11-14
Gospel: John 21:1-19

Scripture Focus

The scene in today's Gospel appears as a commentary upon a statement made by Jesus: "Apart from me you can do nothing." Apart from him their efforts have been fruitless, but now that they are with him, anything is possible. Peter's leadership role is expressed in pastoral imagery. With leadership comes responsibility and a call to imitate the selfless love of Christ. It is summed up in the statement, "Follow me." The risen Lord invites him not only to death but to resurrection. Jesus passed from this world to the Father through death. Those who profess to follow the Lord must take the same route. That is why Jesus is truly "the way."

Life Focus

1. Relate an experience when someone did not give up on you in spite of your past failures.

2. Describe a time when you were affirmed as a person and given a job to finish.

3. How have you felt when someone in your life asked you the same question over and over? What is God repeatedly asking of you in your life right now?

4. Which "sheep" are not being fed well now? What will you do about this in the next two weeks?

5. What does it mean for you when Jesus says to you, "Follow me"? What prevents you from following Jesus?

6. What behaviors or addictions do you need to give up in order for others to recognize Christ in you?

7. What is God repeatedly asking of you in your life right now?

—Archdiocese of Denver
  Queen of Peace Catholic Church
  Denver, Colorado

Fourth Sunday of Easter (C)

Reading I: Acts 13:14, 43-52
Reading II: Revelation 7:9, 14-17
Gospel: John 10:27-30

Scripture Focus

The focus of this Sunday's Gospel is on Jesus as the Good Shepherd. The short talk stresses the unbreakable relationship between Jesus and his sheep. Like all well-tended sheep, they respond only to their shepherd's voice. He knows and loves them, and they respond by following him. He gives them a share in the very life of God, a promise that will never stop. God has given them to Jesus, and there is no snatching them out of God's hand. The statements of ownership are strong proofs that the sheep cannot be taken away from Jesus or God.

Life Focus

1. Right now, where do you experience belonging and having a place? Where do you experience not really belonging?

2. Share one of your stronger experiences of conflict in your life (as a teenager, parent, spouse or employee). How was it resolved?

3. "Birds of a feather flock together." Relate an experience when you realized that you truly belonged to a group. Share your feelings about that experience.

4. Speak of an experience in your life when your sense of belonging was so real that you knew you could count on others to be responsible for you.

—Diocese of St. Paul
  St. John the Baptist Parish
  Fort McMurray, Alberta, Canada

(continued)

91

1. Describe an experience when you felt cared for, felt a sense of belonging, felt connected.

2. Speak of a time in your life when you felt lost. How did you find your way, or how are you handling it now?

3. How do you hear God in your everyday life? What gets in the way?

4. What kind of people do you find yourself following? Why?

5. Who have you been called to lead in some way?

—Archdiocese of Santa Fe
    Santa Fe, New Mexico

Fifth Sunday of Easter (C)

Reading I: Acts 14:21-27
Reading II: Revelation 21:1-5
Gospel: John 13:31-33, 34-35

Scripture Focus

There are many examples in the Bible of farewell speeches. They always include leaving a farewell gift. Jesus addresses his disciples as "my children," like a father would on his deathbed. Jesus' gift is the commandment to "love one another." This is the key to eternal happiness. "Love your neighbor as yourself" had been around for a long time. There was something new in Jesus' command. They were to love each other as Jesus loves. It is to be a totally selfless love. His death on the cross is the highest expression of his love. It is this *love* which identifies the disciples with Jesus. What we believe, how we behave and worship must be motivated by his command to "love one another" as he loves us. This is the necessary mark of a truly Christian community.

Life Focus

1. In what way is yours a truly Christian community? In what way is it not? Where do you fit in?

2. Describe a time in your life when someone close to you went out of your life. What did that person leave behind for you? How did that person affect your life?

3. How do you love someone who is very difficult to love?

4. Tell of a time when your attempts at love were rebuffed.

5. How were you able to resolve a situation with someone you just couldn't love?

—Diocese of La Crosse
    St. Olaf Parish
    Eau Claire, Wisconsin

Sixth Sunday of Easter (C)

Reading I: Acts 15:1-2, 22-29
Reading II: Revelation 21:10-14, 22-23
Gospel: John 14:23-29

Scripture Focus

Both the reading from Acts and the Gospel tell us that Luke was interested in showing the abiding presence of the Lord with the early Christian community. Both groups involved in the dispute in Acts trusted that the Holy Spirit would guide them to the right decision. In the Gospel Jesus includes a promise and a challenge in his farewell. He promises to "make his dwelling place" with them always. The condition for him to be present with all his heart, however, is that they continue to love him and to take his message seriously. Jesus says the message is not just his but also that of the Father. He is the messenger of the Father. He promises to send the Spirit who will stand at their side and teach them all things.

Life Focus

1. Speak of a time when you trusted and experienced true peace.

2. Where do you need peace right now?

3. Relate a situation when you were guided by an influence greater than yourself.

4. On what occasion have you come to realize that your "talents" came from beyond yourself?

5. In what past or present decisions have you needed God's wisdom and guidance?

—Diocese of Phoenix
  Phoenix, Arizona

Seventh Sunday of Easter (C)

Reading I: Acts 7:55-60
Reading II: Revelation 22:12-14, 16-17, 20
Gospel: John 17:20-26

Scripture Focus

Today's Gospel continues Jesus' prayer at the Last Supper. In the first part of the farewell Jesus prayed for himself. In the second part he prays for his disciples. In today's passage he is praying for all disciples of all time. Jesus' prayer for unity means more than a shallow "belonging." It is a deep unity patterned on the unity between the Father and the Son. Jesus wants all his disciples to share the same glory the Father gave to him. This is the destiny meant for all Christians. But it is based on the free acceptance of God's offer of love. It is not a question of knowing *about* God, but of *knowing* him in a deep interpersonal relationship with God. It involves loving and embracing God and all God's daughters and sons.

Life Focus

1. Relate an experience from your life when you felt that your actions were guided by God.

2. Jesus prays "that all may be one." Have you ever felt that oneness with one another, or a oneness with the earth as God's creation?

3. As Jesus prays for us, his disciples today, what is he praying for? What will you do to cooperate with his prayer?

4. Share an experience when you felt "unity" with the Father and the Son, or tell of a time when you needed that "unity."

—Archdiocese of Toronto
  Epiphany of Our Lord
  Scarboro, Ontario, Canada

The Body and Blood of Christ (C)

Reading I: Genesis 14:18-20
Reading II: 1 Corinthians 11:23-26
Gospel: Luke 9:11-17

Scripture Focus

Luke's Gospel stresses Jesus' table fellowship with people of all sorts. This and other themes emerge in his account of Jesus feeding the multitude. (1) When Jesus asks the apostles to give the people something to eat themselves, it is a thinly veiled hint that they are to imitate him in feeding the hungry. (2) His generosity is suggested by the fact that "they all ate until they had enough" and underscored by the quantity of leftovers, enough to fill twelve baskets. (Twelve symbolized all humanity.) Some people at Corinth had forgotten the significance of the Eucharist and were nullifying it by their selfishness. The rich members of the community were turning the common meal into a private bash. Paul reminded them that the Eucharist bonds us to all the people around God's table.

Life Focus

1. When have you felt you were running on empty?

2. Do you hunger in your family, work or community? Name one thing you can do to make a difference.

3. What would make your life complete?

4. Christ related with all types of people. What type of people do you find easy to include in your life? What type of people are easy to exclude?

5. Today, who are the people who do not feel welcome in our Church? Can you take any practical steps to welcome at least one of these people?

—Diocese of San Bernardino
   San Bernardino, California

Trinity Sunday (C)

Reading I: Proverbs 8:22-31
Reading II: Romans 5:1-5
Gospel: John 16:12-15

Scripture Focus

The Gospel reading emphasizes the work of the "Spirit of truth" in the Christian community. Jesus is about to leave his disciples and is making provision for their future. Even though he has more to tell them, they cannot understand it before the death/resurrection event. Only in the light of their experience of the risen Christ will they be able to comprehend its significance. This insight, given by "the Spirit of truth," will guide them throughout the centuries in their efforts to grow in understanding. A striking feature of this passage is its stress on the common working of Jesus, his Father and the Spirit of truth. They possess in common; they act in common.

Life Focus

1. Name a time when suffering and injustice inspired you to seek out the truth.

2. When something is forbidden, we desire to know why it is forbidden or why we are being denied access to something. Relate a time when something that was kept from you motivated you to search and thus deepen your faith.

3. A life filled with constant lies hinders one from the truth. How do you recognize untruth? How do you keep yourself open to the truth?

4. Any attempt to gain understanding of your enemy helps you not to condemn but to find peace in difficult situations. What do you do to try to understand your enemy? When has "understanding your enemy" led to acceptance?

5. When has the experience of being helpless and weak led you to reflect within? How has this reflection helped you face adversity?

—Lithuanian Exchange Students
   Lithuanian Summer Camp
   Camp Neringa, Brattleboro, Vermont

Second Sunday of Ordinary Time (C)

Reading I: Isaiah 62:1-5
Reading II: 1 Corinthians 12:4-11
Gospel: John 2:1-12

Scripture Focus

In the wedding at Cana John tells us the simple story of a wedding, which more importantly, is a "sign." A wedding *is* taking place, not only the one at Cana, but the more important one between God and people. God joins to Israel in the appearance of the Son. When Jesus changes water into wine, he replaces the old order (water) with the new (wine). The astonishing amount of wine (ninety to one hundred fifty gallons) suggests the superabundant blessings of this new age. Here lies the truth behind the wedding scene. Jesus revealed his "glory" and the disciples "saw" and began to believe in him.

Life Focus

1. Who helped bring your faith to life? How do you do this for others?

2. What blessings have come to you beyond what you asked or expected?

3. When were you able to talk to those close to you about who you are and what you believe?

4. Where has the wine run out in your life?

5. Describe a recent "ordinary" event that ended up having extraordinary meaning for you.

—Diocese of Worcester
  St. Augustine Community
  Worcester, Massachusetts

1. Describe a time in your life when letting go of the familiar allowed something new and better to happen.

2. From your personal experience, how has someone filled a need in your life that you were unable to find ways to fill?

—Diocese of Rockville Centre
  Rockville Centre, New York

95

Third Sunday of Ordinary Time (C)

Reading I: Nehemiah 8:2-4, 5-6, 8-10
Reading II: 1 Corinthians 12:12-30
Gospel: Luke 1:1-4—4:14-21

Scripture Focus

This Sunday's Gospel is an introduction. The first part introduces us to the Gospel of Luke; the second introduces the Gospel message into the world. The first four verses of this passage form the prologue to Luke's Gospel. He writes not only to Theophilus (Beloved of God) but to the community of those who believe in Christ. The second introduction is like an inauguration speech by Jesus as he begins his work. Invited to give a talk on the scriptures, in his hometown synagogue, Jesus stands and reads from Isaiah. Anointed by the Spirit, he has been sent to preach the Good News to the poor, the disadvantaged, the exploited. A new age dawns and Isaiah's prophetic words are now fulfilled.

Life Focus

1. From your experience, describe someone who is poor.

2. What is good news to a poor person? Give examples.

3. Give an experience when you were blind to the needs of the poor. Give reasons for your blindness.

4. In the Gospel Jesus announces his work to bring God's kingdom. What is your work?

5. How would you introduce Christ and his teachings to someone who does not know him?

—St. Peter Claver Church
  Kingston, Jamaica

Fourth Sunday of Ordinary Time (C)

Reading I: Jeremiah 1:4-5, 17-19
Reading II: 1 Corinthians 12:31—13:13
Gospel: Luke 4:21-30

Scripture Focus

In today's Gospel initial enthusiasm is followed by growing hostility as Jesus gives evidence of a preferential option for the poor, the outcasts, the sinners. After a violent attempt on his life, he simply walks away. This foreshadows the end of the Gospel when God will raise him from the grip of death. The crowd finds it difficult to accept Jesus as anything but Joseph's son. How could an ordinary human being obtain such wisdom? They reject the very idea that Jesus could be anything other than what they suppose him to be. But Jesus goes on to suggest that even Gentiles will be acceptable to God. At this preaching, many would know a "turning point" in their lives, even as we do whenever we turn to Christ in our own lives.

Life Focus

1. Describe the time or times in your life when you had a sense of God calling you.

2. Jesus pursues the outcasts. Who do you find easy to exclude? Why?

3. Describe how your personal understanding and appreciation of Jesus have changed over the years.

4. Relate an experience when you attempted to make Jesus and his values known to your friends, relatives and companions but were contradicted or laughed at or coldly received by them. What were your thoughts and feelings then?

—Diocese of Honolulu
  St. John Church
  Honolulu, Hawaii

Fifth Sunday of Ordinary Time (C)

Reading I: Isaiah 6:1-2, 3-8
Reading II: 1 Corinthians 15:1-11
Gospel: Luke 5:1-11

Scripture Focus

In today's Gospel we hear Jesus calling the first disciples. Jesus calls unlikely, even unworthy people to follow him, but in response to his assurance of forgiveness, we see a generous response to the call. Even Peter, first among the apostles, is first astonished at the power of Jesus and then overcome by a sense of his own sinfulness. But Jesus overlooks Peter's protests that he is unworthy and calls him beyond that to reach out to others.

Life Focus

1. Relate an experience when you felt a sense of awe or wonder.

2. What do you think God is calling you to do in your life?

3. How is God calling you this week to carry out your mission?

4. Describe an experience when another person helped you overcome fear.

5. When were you asked to do something you couldn't handle? Where did you find the strength?

—Archdiocese of Detroit
   Detroit, Michigan

Sixth Sunday of Ordinary Time (C)

Reading I: Jeremiah 17:5-8
Reading II: 1 Corinthians 15:12, 16-20
Gospel: Luke 6:17, 20-26

Scripture Focus

The "beatitudes" and "woes" in today's Gospel should be looked at together because they balance one another. The poor should not be too easily identified with a social class for the poor are not just the economically poor but also the lowly and oppressed who seek God's will. On the other hand, the rich are not condemned just because they are rich. But their riches can easily make them independent, not needing God or others. And they can begin to believe that they have a right to what they own, that they don't have to notice the poor around them. We are promised happiness and fullness, but we are challenged to keep ourselves humble and our lives simple. Jesus preaches poverty because poverty forces us to trust totally in God. We have to realize that the Kingdom holds the ultimate value.

Life Focus

1. Imagine yourself happy. Where are you? Who is with you? What are you doing? What are you feeling?

2. Speak of an apparent misfortune, "bad luck" or disaster. What was the hidden blessing?

3. Describe a time in your life when you *felt* poor or deprived. What impact do the words of Jesus have on these feelings?

4. What are the things money can't buy?

5. How can your life be simpler? How can you depend more on God? How can you begin to notice poor people?

—Diocese of Wheeling-Charleston
   Catholic Church of the Ascension
   Hurricane, West Virginia

Seventh Sunday of Ordinary Time (C)

Reading I: 1 Samuel 26:2, 7-9, 12-13, 22-23
Reading II: 1 Corinthians 15:45-49
Gospel: Luke 6:27-38

Scripture Focus

Today's reading from Luke's "Sermon on the Plain," a parallel of Matthew's Sermon on the Mount, contains the revolutionary command: Love your enemies. Reacting with violence only breeds more violence. The Christian way rises above getting even: "Do good to those who hate you.... Do to others what you would have them do to you." Love of enemies makes people truly Godlike! Luke's Jesus tells his listeners to be compassionate as God is compassionate. God has already withheld judgment from us. The reward for our compassion will be beyond all measure!

Life Focus

1. Think of an experience in your life when someone mistreated you or someone you love. What was your reaction to that person? How could you better deal with this same situation?

2. Describe a person whom you find it almost impossible to forgive or love. Describe the feelings you cannot change toward this person. Without trying to change the feelings, how can you begin the process of forgiving?

3. Which of these is the hardest for you to do? Which is the easiest? Forgiving others, loving your enemies, not judging others, turning the other cheek, giving willingly and without expecting anything in return?

—Diocese of La Crosse
St. Olaf Parish
Eau Claire, Wisconsin

Eighth Sunday of Ordinary Time (C)

Reading I: Sirach 27:4-7
Reading II: 1 Corinthians 15:54-58
Gospel: Luke 6:39-45

Scripture Focus

Today's Gospel shares with Matthew's Sermon on the Mount the sayings about the speck and plank and the tree and its fruits, which is an indication that they were in the common source used by Luke and Matthew. In every community there are people who are quick to point out other people's faults. This self-righteousness is not only annoying; it is dangerous. It can blind these self-appointed guardians of moral conduct to their own, often serious, shortcomings. They are warned here, in very graphic terms. In the end, the test of one's goodness is one's own conduct.

Life Focus

1. What hinders you from seeing goodness in another? In yourself?

2. In your call to be a disciple, who do you see as your teacher? Where do you seek wisdom? How is Scripture a source of wisdom for you?

3. In light of this gospel message describe an incident in your life when you felt it was necessary to advise/correct another person.

- What were the steps that enabled you to do this?
- How did you feel before, during and after this process?
- What insights did you gain about yourself?

—Diocese of Boise
St. Mary Parish
Boise, Idaho

Ninth Sunday of Ordinary Time (C)

Reading I: 1 Kings 8:41-43
Reading II: Galatians 1:1-2, 6-10
Gospel: Luke 7:1-10

Scripture Focus

In today's Gospel Jesus shows us through the healing of the Centurion's servant just how compassionate God is. Luke, a Gentile himself, writes for a Gentile community. Luke paints the Gentile centurion in flattering colors. The centurion professes his confidence in the power of Jesus' word. All Jesus has to do is "give the order," as he has done many times himself in his position of authority, and the servant will be cured. Jesus praises this remarkable faith. In fact, he very pointedly contrasts it to the lack of faith he encounters among his own people. Luke's story prepares for the movement of the Gospel into the world of the Gentiles. Jews and Gentiles will exist side by side in Christ.

Life Focus

1. Describe a time in your life when you worked with someone not a Christian in performing a good deed or project. Was there anything special about it?

2. Describe a time in your life when you or your small church community overcame fears, anxieties or other obstacles that hindered working with others.

3. If the Lord were to come to your house today, would you feel worthy enough to receive him? If you felt unworthy, would you invite him in anyway?

4. Relate a story when you felt like an outsider.

5. Describe a time when you were awed by the faith and generosity of another.

6. Who are the outsiders in the Church? In your small church community?

7. What in this story challenges you? Consoles you?

—Diocese of Fort Worth
  St. Michael Catholic Community
  Bedford, Texas

Tenth Sunday of Ordinary Time (C)

Reading I: 1 Kings 17:17-24
Reading II: Galatians 1:11-19
Gospel: Luke 7:11-17

Scripture Focus

The Jews of Jesus' time looked forward to Elijah's return. Some felt that he had returned in Jesus. When Jesus encounters a grieving widow in Naim, he restores her son to life, just as Elijah had done in the story we heard from the First Book of Kings. Only God can bring life. Through God's power, Elijah restored the boy's life. Through his power Jesus raised the young man in Naim. We too can rely on God's power. The word of the Lord *does* give life!

Life Focus

1. Recall an impossible situation when there seemed to be no hope of a solution and then the unexpected happened. In what way did new life appear?

2. Describe a time when someone's words to you gave your life new meaning and purpose.

3. Relate an occasion when your words or actions renewed a lost relationship, revived a dead issue or restored hope in a desperate situation.

—Diocese of Rockville Centre
  The Church of the Good Shepherd
  Holbrook, New York

Eleventh Sunday of Ordinary Time (C)

Reading I: 2 Samuel 12:7-10, 13
Reading II: Galatians 2:16, 19-21
Gospel: Luke 7:36—8:3

Scripture Focus

God's Kingdom often is the direct opposite of the world's ways. Today's Gospel shows how differently Jesus acts from what is expected. The Gospel contrasts a respectable man of religion, a Pharisee, with a woman who is a known sinner. The Pharisee keeps his distance from Jesus. The sinner comes close and, in a touching way, offers Jesus extravagant hospitality. Jesus, going against everything considered proper, lets himself be touched intimately and in public by a woman and a sinner. Jesus' story tells why: because her sins are forgiven, she shows great love.

Life Focus

1. When have women taught you forgiveness? Love?

2. Describe things that we see in our community that reveal scorn for weak members.

3. Relate a situation in which your appreciation and gratitude for a person had to be expressed.

4. Who in your life has not held your past against you?

5. Share an experience when you were invited to begin to break the barriers of past hurts. What was your response?

—Diocese of Kalamazoo
   St. Joseph Parish
   Kalamazoo, Michigan

Twelfth Sunday of Ordinary Time (C)

Reading I: Zechariah 12:10-11
Reading II: Galatians 3:26-29
Gospel: Luke 9:18-24

Scripture Focus

In today's Gospel we reach a climax. Jesus will soon start his fateful journey to Jerusalem. He asks the crucial question: "Who do people say I am?" Peter, spokesman for the disciples, recognizes Jesus as the Messiah. Peter had no facts on which to base his declaration, but he did have faith! Immediately Peter and the other disciples are challenged to rethink their definition of Messiah. Jesus is not a military or political figure. He is a suffering, dying and rising Messiah. Jesus clearly tells the disciples and the crowd that there is a cost to being a follower. You must be willing to lose yourself and go where Jesus leads—even if that means changing your thinking and beliefs, or suffering injustice, or loss of comforts. But of course you will be with Jesus.

Life Focus

1. Where do you go for seclusion?

2. If an atheist asked you who Jesus was and why you follow him, what would you say?

3. Share about someone you know who has "taken up a cross" each day. How does this inspire you?

4. Which of Jesus' footsteps would you find it impossible to walk in? Why?

5. In your life, where have you gone or what have you done because of Jesus' lead?

—Diocese of Green Bay
   St. Mary of the Angels Parish
   Green Bay, Wisconsin

Thirteenth Sunday of Ordinary Time (C)

Reading I: 1 Kings 19:16, 19-21
Reading II: Galatians 5:1, 13-18
Gospel: Luke 9:51-62

Scripture Focus

Today's Gospel spells out what it means to follow Jesus, to be his disciple. James and John, "sons of thunder," angry at being rejected by the Samaritans, want to call down fire from heaven to consume Jesus' enemies. Jesus says there is no room for getting even in the Christian way of life. There is to be no violence. Luke develops the theme of discipleship further using three examples. Jesus tells the one who offers to follow him "wherever he goes" of the hardships involved. His strange reply to the man who wants to go home first to bury his father underlines the urgency to get on with proclaiming the reign of God. And finally there is a singleness of purpose involved in being a follower of Jesus. There can be no looking back to what one has left behind.

Life Focus

1. How do you react when someone criticizes you or is hostile to you?

2. When in your life have you been called to change direction (put your hand to a different "plow") because of your desire to be a follower of Jesus?

3. What does it mean to your everyday life to be a follower of Jesus?

4. What is your reaction to being called by Jesus?

—Archdiocese of Indianapolis
  Office of Catholic Education
  Indianapolis, Indiana

Fourteenth Sunday of Ordinary Time (C)

Reading I: Isaiah 66:10-14
Reading II: Galatians 6:14-18
Gospel: Luke 10:1-12, 17-20

Scripture Focus

For centuries God's people longed for a messiah. They yearned for someone who would bring about God's reign, a time of peace and blessings. The prophets had an unshakable faith in God's reign and communicated that confidence to the people. It is this reign that Jesus preached and began. He commissions the seventy-two disciples to proclaim the coming of this reign. The peace of God's reign is made possible through Jesus' life, death and resurrection. It is the fulfillment of all humanity's hopes. The disciples are successful because they are agents of God's grace. That they have been chosen as instruments of that grace is the real reason for rejoicing.

Life Focus

1. How does Jesus ask you to spread the gospel in the world today? What obstacles do you see in your path? What do you need to do to overcome these obstacles?

2. When have you felt like a lamb walking among wolves?

3. What instructions that you received early in your faith life are still valid and useful today?

—Archdiocese of San Francisco
  Most Holy Redeemer Parish
  San Francisco, California

Fifteenth Sunday of Ordinary Time (C)

Reading I: Deuteronomy 30:10-14
Reading II: Colossians 1:15-20
Gospel: Luke 10:25-37

Scripture Focus

In today's Gospel two questions are addressed to Jesus by a legal expert and Jesus answers both by posing a further question. The answer to the second question takes a bit more time. Jesus tells a shocking story. The story is shocking because the Samaritans, who were descended from Jews who had intermarried with pagans, were hated by Jews. So, the good Samaritan looks after someone who despises him. After the story, Jesus poses a counter-question, which really changes the original question from "Who is my neighbor?" to "What is involved in my being a neighbor?" The reluctant answer is "The one who treated him with compassion." And Jesus says, "Then go and do the same."

Life Focus

1. In the parable of the Good Samaritan, which of the four characters do you identify with? Explain.

2. Speak of a time when you felt second best or excluded. Who was or was not a Good Samaritan to you?

3. Who are the people in this world who couldn't teach you a thing?

4. Tell of a time you were a good neighbor to a stranger.

5. Describe an occasion when you did *not* help a person who needed you.

6. When has a person you least expected shown you the way?

7. Who or when do you find it easy to pass by? Why?

—Archdiocese of San Antonio
   San Antonio, Texas

Sixteenth Sunday of Ordinary Time (C)

Reading I: Genesis 18:1-10
Reading II: Colossians 1:24-28
Gospel: Luke 10:38-42

Scripture Focus

In today's first reading we get a glimpse of the importance of hospitality in the desert. The Gospel continues this theme of hospitality. Martha prepares the meal in the kitchen while Mary sits at the Lord's feet. Martha takes exception to Mary's action, but Mary is being hospitable in her own way. Jesus teaches Martha to balance her work with a bit of listening. It is not that her work isn't important, but action by itself can easily become mindless busyness. It's a question of balancing priorities. Notice that both women are close frinds of Jesus and they are listed as doing the work of disciples.

Life Focus

1. Who are you most like, Mary or Martha? Tell of an experience from your life to show this. How can you develop the other side of yourself?

2. Tell of an experience in your life when your attention was focused on the less important thing in a situation.

3. What are the contributions of women to your small church community? To your parish?

4. As an individual what do you do to prepare yourself to listen to Christ? Do you have a special time or place for listening?

5. Who, more than anyone, makes you feel at home? How? How can you show this kind of hospitality to others this week?

6. How can your life be more centered and clear?

—Archdiocese of Dubuque
   St. Cecilia Parish
   Ames, Iowa

Seventeenth Sunday of Ordinary Time (C)

Reading I: Genesis 18:20-32
Reading II: Colossians 2:12-14
Gospel: Luke 11:1-13

Scripture Focus

In today's Gospel Luke gives us his version of the Lord's Prayer, slightly different in wording from Matthew's version. It would seem that Jesus taught his disciples *how* to pray without giving them a precise formula. The central request is for the coming of God's reign. Physical nourishment is necessary as people await the reign, and Luke suggests that it will be a long wait by adding the significant "each day." One attitude is singled out: mutual forgiveness modeled on God's own forgiveness. One quality of prayer is stressed: perseverance. Eventual success is assured, and in the process one stays in touch with God.

Life Focus

1. When has there seemed to be no answer to your prayer? What has been your response? Describe the change in yourself.

2. From your experience, what keeps you praying or not praying?

3. We all need "daily bread." What does this *bread* include for you?

4. How are you affected when you are slow to forgive?

5. Who in your life do you need to forgive (include yourself)?

6. Reflect on a time when your prayer was answered in a different way than you expected.

—Archdiocese of Omaha
  St. Stanislaus Parish
  Omaha, Nebraska

Eighteenth Sunday of Ordinary Time (C)

Reading I: Ecclesiastes 1:2; 2:21-23
Reading II: Colossians 3:1-5, 9-11
Gospel: Luke 12:13-21

Scripture Focus

The "Parable of the Rich Fool," told only by Luke, contrasts those who place their trust in material possessions with those who recognize their complete dependence on God. The parable challenges us to rethink our priorities and our attitudes about wealth. It also calls us to make a decision about possessiveness and then act on our decision. By refusing to decide the case, Jesus forces the two brothers to come to their own decisions. The parable challenges us to "seek first the reign of God."

Life Focus

1. Tell about a time when material goods failed to satisfy you.

2. How can you store up "riches in the sight of God" that you can "take with you"?

3. Tell how "avoiding greed in all its forms" can help you shape your everyday life.

4. You know people who spend years planning for their retirement and something goes wrong. What can you do today that will last no matter what happens?

—Diocese of Kalamazoo
  St. John the Evangelist Church
  Benton Harbor, Michigan

(continued)

1. What helps you find a balance between taking reasonable care of yourself and hearing the needs all around you?

2. Recall how wanting to control something or someone really controlled you.

3. Do you take time to visit with people and with God? What things tend to "get in the way"?

4. Drawing upon your experience, track down the various ways you are being pressured to put your security in the possession of material goods.

—Archdiocese of Edmonton
    Our Lady of Perpetual Help Parish
    Sherwood Park, Alberta, Canada

Nineteenth Sunday of Ordinary Time (C)

Reading I: Wisdom 18:6-9
Reading II: Hebrews 11:1-2, 8-19
Gospel: Luke 12:32-48

Scripture Focus

The theme of constant and confident waiting comes up again and again in Luke's Gospel: "Do not live in fear, little flock." The kingdom *is* theirs, and their treasure lies not in amassed possessions but in what they share with the unfortunate. Their watchword must be vigilance. The Lord's coming is certain; only its time is undetermined. It could happen any time, so don't get careless. The beautiful figure of the master putting on an apron and waiting on his faithful servants will be repeated in Luke's Last Supper scene, when Jesus identifies himself in these terms: "I am among you as the one who serves." It is also a serious reminder that we must be faithful during the master's "absence." Those in positions of leadership—in answer to Peter's question—have to be especially careful. They must not turn leadership into self-serving domination. "More will be asked of a person to whom more has been entrusted."

Life Focus

1. Relate a time in your life, or the life of someone you know, when the search for wealth resulted in the loss of much greater joy.

2. Describe an incident from your life when faith allowed you to attempt something that common sense alone would have cautioned against.

3. What helps to keep you "vigilant"? How do you pay attention to the Lord?

4. What have you done so far with what "has been entrusted to you"?

—Diocese of Green Bay
    St. Mary of the Angels Parish
    Green Bay, Wisconsin

Twentieth Sunday of Ordinary Time (C)

Reading I: Jeremiah 38:4-6, 8-10
Reading II: Hebrews 12:1-4
Gospel: Luke 12:49-53

Scripture Focus

Jesus began his ministry by announcing the reign of God and liberation from sin and suffering. His words and deeds stir up much controversy. Pressed, he never shies from a dispute. He must be faithful to himself, to God. He is often blunt. He says exactly what he means. The heat of conflict rises between Jesus and his opponents. The coupling of the Jeremiah story with Luke's narrative amplifies Jesus' warning about controversy and division. God's ways are not our ways. Nor do we always like what we hear from the Lord. Stay close to the word of God. But know that God's word is like a two-edged sword that "penetrates and divides soul and spirit, joint and marrow." God's word always cuts to the truth. And in doing so, it sometimes severs family ties, community ties. The Lord asks fidelity.

Life Focus

1. Share an experience when you felt called to do or say something "right," but it caused great conflict in your home, work, neighborhood, etc.

2. Recall a time when you felt that what was asked of you was difficult, but you did it out of love of God.

3. What do you find difficult about following the word of the Lord?

—Archdiocese of Detroit
 St. Elizabeth Ann Seton Parish
 Troy, Michigan

1. Relate an experience when doing the right thing caused you trouble or discord. Would you do it again? Where did you find the courage?

2. Is there any way that certain persons or events have ignited a fire in you?

3. Where might you risk some divisions within yourself or with others right now for the sake of a fuller life? What keeps you back?

—Dioceses of Lansing, Saginaw, Kalamazoo
 Lansing, Michigan

Twenty-First Sunday of Ordinary Time (C)

Reading I: Isaiah 66:18-21
Reading II: Hebrews 12:5-7, 11-13
Gospel: Luke 13:22-30

Scripture Focus

Luke, the Gentile, is very interested in God's all-embracing love, a love not limited to certain ethnic or religious groups. In the Gospel Jesus is on his way to Jerusalem. Those with him want to know if those who will be saved are few in number. Jesus was not about to set limits on God's saving power. He was concerned that they use God's power. They are to know that God's generosity must be matched by generosity on their part. Going through "a narrow door" is difficult; one has to work at it. It isn't like slipping through a wide, open passageway in the midst of a large crowd. There is to be a personal, practical response to God's invitation.

Life Focus

1. Going through a "narrow door" is difficult; one has to work at it. In order to make it through the narrow door, what changes do you need to make in your life that you have been putting off?

2. God loves all people, even the ones you find most unacceptable! What will you do about that?

3. Jesus is saying that people are not saved by being members of a certain group (ethnic, religious, etc.) but by acting on a commitment. As a Catholic, how do you feel about this?

—Diocese of Rockford
 Sts. Peter and Paul Church
 Cary, Illinois

1. Describe a time in your life when you felt you had it all together, only to find out you were really off track.

2. Recall an incident in your life when you missed something important because you were too self-centered.

3. Name a time when you took the easy way out, instead of doing the better course of action.

—Diocese of Tulsa
 Tulsa, Oklahoma

Twenty-Second Sunday of Ordinary Time (C)

Reading I: Sirach 3:17-18, 20, 28-29
Reading II: Hebrews 12:18-19, 22-24
Gospel: Luke 14:1, 7-14

Scripture Focus

The setting for today's Gospel passage is another meal. This setting provides the material for Jesus' teaching. The lessons from both parables look to what should be done in order to be at the heavenly banquet in the Father's house. We must be willing to accept our strengths and weaknesses. The weaknesses are the way we come to depend on God and one another. Those who are truly humble will also be willing to come to the aid of the poor because they know that they, too, are poor. This parable prepares us for eternal happiness, as opposed to immediate self-gratification and repayment for favors done.

Life Focus

1. Recall a situation when you put someone else first and when someone put you first.

2. Relate a recent experience when you felt obligated to pay back a gesture of goodwill. What was the outcome?

3. How can you practice giving yourself or your possessions without expecting anything in return?

4. How do you deal with the "beggars, crippled, lame and blind" in this world? Who are they for you?

—Diocese of San Diego
   Our Lady of Perpetual Help Church
   Lakeside, California

1. During this week, how can you use your talents and God's wisdom to make God known?

2. During this week, how can we as a community together use our talents and God's knowledge to proclaim God's name?

—Catechist Training Center Fissoa
   Kavieng, New Ireland Proving
   Papua, New Guinea

Twenty-Third Sunday of Ordinary Time (C)

Reading I: Wisdom 9:13-18
Reading II: Philemon 9-10, 12-17
Gospel: Luke 14:25-33

Scripture Focus

In today's Gospel Jesus tells "a great crowd" the cost of discipleship. To be asked to turn their backs on their nearest and dearest certainly got their attention. Jesus was not asking people to be cold and to turn away from family. He was saying that when even loved ones turn hostile, disciples have to make a choice. Jesus insists that following him means taking up one's cross. The cross will mean different things in people's lives. Whatever the suffering, it should be accepted bravely. To follow him means to follow all the way. Jesus is asking, "Can you afford to follow me?"

Life Focus

1. Name any way that a commitment to follow Christ has affected your decisions.

2. Who has been faithful to you at a real personal cost?

3. Name some aspects of your life that might get in the way of following God.

4. Relate an experience when it was difficult to be a Catholic/Christian in today's world.

—Archdiocese of Melbourne
  Melbourne, Victoria
  Australia

Twenty-Fourth Sunday of Ordinary Time (C)

Reading I: Exodus 32:7-11, 13-14
Reading II: 1 Timothy 1:12-17
Gospel: Luke 15:1-32

Scripture Focus

Luke keeps assuring his readers of God's amazing acceptance of sinners. This conviction is central, of course, to all New Testament writings. God makes the first move, even before the sinner is ready to return. Luke recounts three parables to respond to the snobbery of some of the Pharisees and scribes. Jesus directs these three parables at the self-righteous people, the people who think God must follow their rules. Such people think they determine whom and how God will forgive. But Jesus says God follows God's own rules. Christians are being told not to imitate the religious "snobs" of Jesus' day. They must let God be God and not presume to tell God who can be saved and how people must be saved.

Life Focus

1. Speak of an experience of forgiveness you never thought possible.

2. Relate a time when you felt lost and someone reached out or did not reach out to you.

3. Name an experience that made you proud to be a son or daughter.

4. In these parables, with which person or image do you identify? Why?

5. When have you received more than you deserved?

—Diocese of Rockhampton
  Rockhampton, Queensland
  Australia

(continued)

1. Do you ever make up rules for God to follow like the elder son did? What is the result?

2. Think of a time when you asked God for your inheritance like the prodigal son did.

3. Who have you forgiven? From whom do you need to receive forgiveness?

—Diocese of Madison
  St. Bernard Parish
  Middleton, Wisconsin

Twenty-Fifth Sunday of Ordinary Time (C)

Reading I: Amos 8:4-7
Reading II: 1 Timothy 2:1-8
Gospel: Luke 16:1-13

Scripture Focus

The point of the parable in today's Gospel is that Christians should exercise at least as much clever thinking in the pursuit of good as this fellow did in the pursuit of ill-gotten gain. Luke goes on to suggest to his audience that they are to use their money in a way that will merit God's blessing, for example, by sharing with the poor. One has to be concerned about money, but a thin line divides concern and being controlled. When one steps over that line and *gives oneself* to money, one becomes its slave. Quite simply, "you cannot *give yourself* to God and to money."

Life Focus

1. Relate an experience in your life when someone did something for you without expecting something in return.

2. What gives you a feeling of security?

3. Describe a time in your life when your personal needs overrode the needs of others.

4. Looking back on your life, what achievements or struggles made you feel worthwhile?

5. Describe an experience of trying to balance your responsibilities in this world and in the next.

—Diocese of Townsville
  Townsville, Queensland
  Australia

(continued)

1. At what times in your life was your desire to help others the highest?

2. How much does money play a part in your life?

3. From your observation and/or experience, how is the Gospel situation true of the present times? Do you identify more with the manager, the boss or the debtor?

4. How can you use your wealth and talents to help God's work?

—Diocese of San Jose
   St. Maria Goretti Parish
   San Jose, California

1. Name some valuables in your life that money can't buy.

2. Relate an experience when you got ahead or got something at the expense of another—or chose not to.

3. Recall a time in your life when a material possession affected a relationship.

—Diocese of Kansas City-St. Joseph
   Kansas City, Missouri

Twenty-Sixth Sunday of Ordinary Time (C)

Reading I: Amos 6:1, 4-7
Reading II: 1 Timothy 6:11-16
Gospel: Luke 16:19-31

Scripture Focus

The Gospel parable tells the familiar story of an insensitive rich man and a poor beggar whom everyone ignores. Jesus addresses this parable to the Pharisees. They had just "sneered at him." They didn't like his words to them: "You cannot serve God and mammon" (the material possessions of the world). Luke points out that the rich man did not kick or injure Lazarus. He simply stepped around him and wouldn't look at him. He treated him as a *non-person*. The message here is nothing new. As Abraham points out, Moses and the prophets consistently preached a message of concern for others. And the Gospel writer knows that even Jesus' own resurrection from the dead is not enough to convince some people to change their ways. Will we listen to one who has risen from the dead?

Life Focus

1. How do you feel when you see a street person? Does it make a difference if you are by yourself or with a group?

2. In what ways do you identify with the *rich* person in the Gospel? In what ways do you identify with the *poor* person in the Gospel?

3. Who are the people you have never really seen? How can that change in the next two weeks?

4. Have you ever felt like a "non-person"? How did this affect you? How does it affect the way you trust others?

—Diocese of Kansas City-St. Joseph
   Guardian Angels Parish
   Kansas City, Missouri

Twenty-Seventh Sunday of Ordinary Time (C)

Reading I: Habakkuk 1:2-3, 2:2-4
Reading II: 2 Timothy 1:6-8, 13-14
Gospel: Luke 17:5-10

Scripture Focus

The first reading calls for deep trust that God's plan is happening and will soon be completed. In the Gospel reading the disciples ask for an increase in faith. Jesus is saying they do not need to be heroes. An ordinary amount of trust in God's help will help them accomplish great things. Transplanting a sycamore tree into the sea is a highly exaggerated example. It serves, however, to make the point: "What is impossible for human beings is possible for God" (Luke 18:27).

Life Focus

1. How have you experienced the struggle between doing what God wants and doing what you want?

2. How have you reacted when asked to do more than what you really wanted to do?

3. Describe an experience when you received less recognition than you expected.

—Diocese of Crookston
  St. Joseph Catholic Church
  Bagley, Minnesota

1. Relate an experience when God asked "too much" of you.

2. Describe a recent time when you did something without expecting a reward, or a time when you did not!

—Diocese of La Crosse
  La Crosse, Wisconsin

Twenty-Eighth Sunday of Ordinary Time (C)

Reading I: 2 Kings 5:14-17
Reading II: 2 Timothy 2:8-13
Gospel: Luke 17:11-19

Scripture Focus

The readings for this Sunday deal with leprosy. In biblical times there was only one way to control the disease: Isolate the person with leprosy from *all* aspects of society. Those with leprosy were cut off from everything: family, friends, employment and worship. No one would dare to approach them and they dared approach no one. Both readings use this dreaded disease to point up the power of God to work wonders through ordinary means. Only one of the men cured by Jesus had the decency to go back and thank him. Only one of them fully realized what had taken place. His is the complete healing, his is the deepest faith. This man, a Samaritan, was an outcast due to both his leprosy and his ethnic background. Luke uses this story to point out the ingratitude of Jesus' own people in contrast to the gratitude and faith of Gentiles.

Life Focus

1. How do you best show your gratitude to God? To others?

2. Share a time when you were aware or are aware that you did not show gratitude to God or to others.

3. What are the "leprosies" in your life that need to be healed? Zero in on one in particular.

—Archdiocese of Detroit
  St. Elizabeth Ann Seton Parish
  Troy, Michigan

(continued)

111

1. Recall an experience of being accepted when you were feeling rejected.

2. Relate an experience when you felt like a stranger and someone welcomed you.

3. Speak of a person you know who is truly grateful.

—Diocese of Rockville Centre
  Rockville Centre, New York

Twenty-Ninth Sunday of Ordinary Time (C)

Reading I: Exodus 17:8-13
Reading II: 2 Timothy 3:14—4:2
Gospel: Luke 18:1-8

Scripture Focus

Luke's Gospel is noted for his preaching on prayer. He also pays great attention to women, especially poor women. Widows were dependent on other men in the family. A widow had no state aid, nor could she work. If she had no one to help her, she had to beg. The widow in this story comes to the judge to help her get her rights. Since she was too poor to offer a bribe, he at first ignores her. But she kept insisting on her rights. The judge was afraid of her. He eventually gave in. If such a worthless judge would answer such pleas, would the loving God do any less? On the contrary, says Jesus, God will respond to people. God will bring them swift justice. Will God find people with the same unconquerable trust as this widow?

Life Focus

1. In what ways has your parish community imitated God's compassion by responding to the cries for justice in neighborhood, country and world?

2. Reflect and share an instance when ongoing prayer in your life carried you through a difficult time.

3. How often in your prayer life are you persistent enough to ignore the answer you want to hear and persistent enough to heed the answer God wants you to hear?

4. What are you doing to bring about God's justice in the world? In your own small world?

5. Who has "nagged" you into doing the right thing or into becoming the person you could be?

—Diocese of London
  Office of RENEW
  London, Ontario, Canada

Thirtieth Sunday of Ordinary Time (C)

Reading I: Sirach 35:12-14, 16-18
Reading II: 2 Timothy 4:6-8, 16-18
Gospel: Luke 18:9-14

Scripture Focus

God is attentive to the prayers of those who have no one else to turn to. These outcasts of society realize that God is their only hope and so, when they pray, they really *pray*. Their prayer comes truly from the heart that acknowledges God's goodness and kindness. The prayer of the tax collector in the Gospel is an example of such prayer. The tax collector simply asks God's mercy for his sinfulness. Jesus heartily approves this form of prayer, the prayer of the lowly which "pierces the clouds." The Pharisee is trapped in his own self-righteousness toward prayer, toward God, toward his fellow Jews and toward himself.

Life Focus

1. When do you identify with characteristics of the Pharisee? When do you identify with characteristics of the tax collector?

2. Relate an experience when you reached out to someone very different from you.

3. When has a simple person, perhaps an outcast, been able to teach you something important?

4. Where are you working too hard at something? Where aren't you working hard enough? What will you do about that soon?

—Archdiocese of Seattle
St. Anthony Parish
Renton, Washington

1. When have you done the right things for the wrong reasons?

2. Recall an experience when admitting a wrong was one of the best things you ever did.

3. Speak of a time when you felt helpless and had to rely on someone.

4. Who are the people we consider not as good as us?

—Archdiocese of Edmonton
Diocese of Calgary
Alberta, Canada

1. In the last few months, how have you experienced failure and how have you reacted?

2. Describe an experience when you felt humble enough to see things differently.

—Diocese of Yakima
Yakima, Washington

Thirty-First Sunday of Ordinary Time (C)

Reading I: Wisdom 11:22—12:1
Reading II: 2 Thessalonians 1:11—2:2
Gospel: Luke 19:1-10

Scripture Focus

Luke is the only evangelist who records the incident about the tax collector, Zacchaeus. Last Sunday's Gospel showed God's acceptance of the sinful tax collector. Today's Gospel provides a concrete example of how repentance is worked out in reality. With total, unconditional acceptance of Zacchaeus, Jesus actually goes into the sinner's house to eat with him. The tax collector is touched by Jesus' love and is willing to rid himself of the worldly possessions that displace God's love. Jesus responds by calling him a "son of Abraham." And Zacchaeus opens his heart to God's invitation and responds with grateful love.

Life Focus

1. What would you do if Jesus came to your house unexpectedly?

2. Who has taken notice of you and taken time for you when you were little noticed or cared for?

—Diocese of Venice
   Fort Meyers, Florida

1. Tell about a time when you accepted someone *as is* and thereby brought about a change in them. Or vice-versa!

2. Zacchaeus did all he could to get a better look at Jesus. What do you do in your life to get to know Jesus better?

—Archdiocese of Detroit
   St. Elizabeth Ann Seton Parish
   Troy, Michigan

1. Relate an experience when someone made a difference in your life simply by accepting you just the way you are.

2. Recall a time in your life when you were given a second chance.

—Archdiocese of Denver
   Denver, Colorado

Thirty-Second Sunday of Ordinary Time (C)

Reading I: Maccabees 7:1-2, 9-14
Reading II: 2 Thessalonians 2:16—3:5
Gospel: Luke 20:27-38

Scripture Focus

In this passage we find Jesus teaching in the temple. The Sadducees, who believed in the absolute authority of the law, approached Jesus with a question about the law. These Sadducees belonged to a group who did not accept the Jewish tradition that believed in the resurrection of the dead. They objected to those who believed that any afterlife was merely a continuation of earthly life. None of us know exactly what to expect after death, but we do have the promise of eternal life and we believe in the fullness of that life.

Life Focus

1. How do you feel about meeting your spouse, mother or father after you all have died?

2. Tell of a time you tried to convince a person of something you believed, but he or she did not. Were you successful? Why or why not?

3. Tell of your first experience with death.

4. Write down three things that you believe about life after death. What is the strongest feeling you have about these?

—Diocese of Fort Wayne-South Bend
  St. John the Evangelist Church
  Goshen, Indiana

Thirty-Third Sunday of Ordinary Time (C)

Reading I: Malachi 3:19-20
Reading II: 2 Thessalonians 3:7-12
Gospel: Luke 21:5-19

Scripture Focus

As we approach the end of the Church year, the liturgy directs our thoughts to the end of time itself. For Jews and Christians this implies victory over all forces of evil, even death itself. A common theme in the writings about this end time is that it will be a time of crisis, a time of decision. Luke's main theme is that it will do no good to try to predict the end time. For followers of Jesus, the important thing is to believe that God will be with them no matter what happens: "You will be hated by all because of my name, but not a hair on your head will be destroyed. By your perseverance you will secure your lives."

Life Focus

1. Describe a time in your life when you had to persevere in order to stand up for what you believed to be right.

2. With wars, famine, suffering, etc., how do you find God's love and trust in your life?

3. Speak of a time in your life when a crisis occurred and you were fearful. How did you get the courage to bounce back?

—Diocese of Albany
  St. Patrick Parish
  Albany, New York

(continued)

115

1. Name an experience when you realized God was in control of your life.

2. Think of a time in your life when you felt everything falling apart. Where did you find support?

3. Describe an experience in your life when others put you down for one of your beliefs.

—Diocese of Rockford
  Rockford, Illinois

Solemnity of Christ the King (C)

Reading I: 2 Samuel 5:1-3
Reading II: Colossians 1:12-20
Gospel: Luke 23:35-43

Scripture Focus

During his adult life Jesus was often put down because he "welcomed sinners and ate with them." Now he is condemned to die with criminals. The man we have come to know as the good thief turns to Jesus and calls him simply by name, "Jesus," and begs only to be "remembered." By doing so he simply acknowledges the inscription on the cross and that Jesus has a kingdom to enter. The thief gets more than he ever asked for: He will enter paradise on that very day. In a word, the criminal was *saved* by Jesus the "savior." The good thief's plea becomes a ray of hope for all, by turning in faith to him who came as a "savior."

Life Focus

1. What helps you believe that Jesus remembers you?

2. How does this Gospel give you hope of being saved?

3. What is lacking in you when you are unable to respond to those suffering unjustly?

—Archdiocese of Boston
  Sisters of St. Francis of Assisi
  Boston, Massachusetts

1. Relate an experience when you received a gift you didn't deserve.

2. Speak of a time when you stood silently witnessing the pain of another.

3. From your experience, describe a time when you failed to respond to someone being unjustly treated.

4. When were you treated unjustly and everyone kept silent?

—Diocese of Norwich
  Norwich, Connecticut

Appendix A:
Small Church Communities in the United States

Diocese of Albany, New York

St. Patrick Parish, Albany. St. Patrick, the sixth oldest parish in the city of Albany, is located in the inner city. It is part of the "Center City Cluster," a group of five parishes and three apostolates working together to serve the people. There are four small church communities with a total membership of thirty-eight men and women.

Diocese of Allentown, Pennsylvania

St. John the Baptist Church, Whitehall. St. John the Baptist Church consists of six hundred families, mostly blue collar, living in the suburbs of Allentown. Sixty people ranging in age from twenty-eight to sixty-five are involved in small church experiences. All parish activities include a time for reflection and faith sharing.

Archdiocese of Anchorage, Alaska

Friends of Jesus Prayer Group, Anchorage. The Archdiocese of Anchorage has a primarily Caucasian population, with some Hispanics, Koreans, Filipinos and blacks. The archdiocese supports the concept of small church communities but is having a difficult time getting parishes to move in this direction. The parishes that have small church communities are doing well.

Archdiocese of Atlanta, Georgia

St. Thomas Aquinas Church, Alpharetta. St. Thomas is a huge suburban parish on the edge of Atlanta. The population consists of transplanted northern Catholics, many of whom are young families with children. St. Thomas is serious about the importance of small communities and the need to reflect on the priorities of everyday life.

Archdiocese of Baltimore, Maryland

St. Joseph Catholic Community, Sykesville. St. Joseph Catholic Community, located in a rapidly growing area of central Maryland, includes nineteen hundred families, mainly middle class and white from a rural/suburban background. Education ranges from high school graduates to master's degrees; careers include both professionals and homemakers. This parish is staffed by Marianists who will continue to move the parish in the direction of small church communities.

St. Isaac Jogues, Baltimore. St. Isaac Jogues is a typical suburban parish of eighteen hundred families located five miles north of Baltimore. Celebrating its twenty-fifth anniversary in 1993, the parish includes many younger, middle- and upper-class families who seek to pass on the faith to their children. Small communities do Scripture study and outreach to the poor of the metropolitan area.

Diocese of Baton Rouge, Louisiana

Holy Rosary Parish, St. Amont. Holy Rosary Parish, located in a rural community, has a membership of 1,660 families. Many parishioners are employed in plants and industrial jobs doing shift work. One hundred-sixty parishioners are in small communities and love it.

Diocese of Bismarck, North Dakota

Spirit of Life Parish, Mandan. Spirit of Life Parish, located about ten miles east of Bismarck, is a modern prayerful parish trying to make small church communities central to its life. Spirit of Life is typical of the many small parishes in North Dakota. Families have lived here for generations but may not talk about their faith with each other or help one another to connect their faith with their daily struggles.

Diocese of Boise, Idaho

St. Mary Parish, Boise. These questions were formulated by a small community in St. Mary Parish. The group consists of single people, single parents, married couples with and without children at home, and widowed people. Each person's background and experience adds a rich dimension to the group.

Archdiocese of Boston, Massachusetts

Sisters of St. Francis of Assisi, Boston. The Archdiocese of Boston is basically a conservative diocese with pockets of liberal parishes mostly in suburban areas. Older parishioners have Irish, Italian or French Canadian roots. Newer members of the urban community tend to be Asian or Hispanic. The older groupings are integrated into the existing parish communities, while the newer groups seek community within their own cultures. This tends to separate some larger urban parishes into two or more communities: Anglo, Hispanic, Asian.

Diocese of Brooklyn, New York

The residential area of this totally urban diocese consists primarily of old apartment buildings. The newest immigrants are Spanish-speaking Puerto Ricans and French-speaking Haitians. Some neighborhoods are dangerous, and small communities may meet only on the same floor of an apartment house. Many social problems exist, but the people have solid values and are struggling to make the best of things. Small communities are happening in several parishes.

Diocese of Brownsville, Texas

St. Paul Church, Mission. The Diocese of Brownsville consists of many Mexicans and second- and third-generation Mexican-Americans. A large number of military personnel stationed at the nearby bases live in and belong to St. Paul Church. St. Paul is trying to make small church communities the basic direction of the diocese.

Diocese of Buffalo, New York

St. Catherine of Siena Parish, West Seneca. St. Catherine, located in a Buffalo suburb, has twelve hundred families, many living outside parish bounds. At the time the faith questions were submitted, the small group consisted of four married couples and five singles, forty to sixty years old.

Diocese of Camden, New Jersey

Four parishes in the diocese are actively pursuing the concept of restructuring the parish. They meet four times a year for an Alliance meeting. Many other parishes have small groups meeting as a result of the RENEW process. The recent diocesan synod mentioned small communities as a direction for the future.

Archdiocese of Chicago, Illinois

The changing ethnic makeup of Chicago's neighborhoods and the movement of Catholics out of the city has forced the painful choice of closing and merging parishes. Yet the archdiocese continues with practical parish renewal and a leadership that is close to its people. There have been two workshops for parishes considering restructuring into small church communities.

Archdiocese of Cincinnati, Ohio

By the year 2000, projections say that the archdiocese will have one-half of its present number of priests. The kind of church that has worked so well here will need a new form.

Precious Blood Church, Dayton. Precious Blood Church, established in 1950, is an urban/suburban/rural middle-class parish of more than one thousand families that is staffed by members of the Society of the Precious Blood. Dayton is a stable, midwestern, German middle-class city. Several parishes are restructuring into small church communities.

St. Francis of Assisi Parish, Centerville. St. Francis is a Christian community of 1,130 families gathered from Belbrook, Kettering and Centerville, all suburbs of Dayton. The parish is made up of retired people and young families caught up in the whirlwind of work, school, Church and community activities.

Middletown-Franklin, Ohio. Middletown has a population of forty-five thousand and is located between Cincinnati and Dayton. In June, 1991, three parishes merged into one.

Diocese of Cleveland, Ohio

The see city of Cleveland, a large industrial city on Lake Erie, faces a decline of ethnic neighborhoods and job losses similar to other major cities. The rest of the diocese includes medium and large cities and rural areas. Life is no longer centered around the parish, especially for younger Catholic families. Much time is spent making a living with both parents working. A number of parish renewal programs are being tried.

St. Barnabas Church, Northfield. The parishioners of St. Barnabas are primarily middle-class Americans from diverse ethnic backgrounds who have chosen to live in a semirural community. The people are plagued by daily concerns of unemployment, job stress and rearing children in today's society. The parish has been working toward small church communities for a number of years.

Our Lady Help of Christians, Litchfield. A five-member team of priests, sisters and lay ministers staffs three parishes in this rural, farming area. Committed to small church communities, the entire staff spent three days at a retreat on restructuring parishes.

Lorain, Ohio. Five parishes participated in a workshop for structuring parishes into small church communities. Lorain is a blue-collar working city. A number of industrial plants have shut down completely or partially and unemployment is high. The older city parishes have an aging population, and younger families live farther from the city center. This is Middle America with strong family and work values and a large percentage of Catholics.

Diocese of Corpus Christi, Texas

St. Cyril and Methodius Church, Corpus Christi. Eighteen hundred families are registered. The parish has seven small faith communities, averaging ten members per group. The questions were formulated by a Hispanic community called *Paloma Blanca.*

Diocese of Crookston, Minnesota

St. Joseph Catholic Church, Bagley. St. Joseph with its 175 Catholic households (many of them elderly and most not economically well off) is located in the middle of the diocese. Parishioners are open to lay ministry because of their natural practicality and willingness to take the initiative to get things done, says Sister Joanne Johnson, C.S.J., pastoral administrator. The people who belong to small faith-sharing groups wish more adults could experience the strength of prayer and support that come from small groups.

Archdiocese of Denver, Colorado

The Archdiocese of Denver is culturally and ethnically diverse because of the contrast between urban, suburban, rural and mountain communities, and the farm and ranch lands of the eastern plains.

Queen of Peace Catholic Church, Aurora. Queen of Peace, located in the heart of Aurora, is nestled on the Great Plains bordering Denver to the east and south. It is the second largest parish in the archdiocese with registered families numbering forty-five hundred and growing. Every age, occupation and economic or ethnic group is represented. The twenty-two small church communities here are a direct result of the parish's active prayer apostolate and commitment to serving the poor.

Light of the World Catholic Parish, Littleton. Light of the World Parish is a large (twenty-six hundred households), progressive, suburban parish located in the rapidly growing southwest part of the Denver metro area. The questions were composed by members of a small church community consisting of twelve people with diverse cultural and ethnic backgrounds who have been meeting for approximately two years. This parish models restructuring to other parishes.

Archdiocese of Detroit, Michigan

The see city of Detroit is eighty percent black and poor. The suburbs are a mix of economic levels. This has always been a town with generous, hardworking European immigrants. Downsizing of auto companies has led to high unemployment. The city and suburbs need to cooperate more closely. Churches offer a way to bridge the gap. The few parishes pursuing small church communities will be demonstration parishes to teach others.

St. Elizabeth Ann Seton Parish, Troy. St. Elizabeth is a parish of seven hundred families, mostly middle-class and white. Usually both parents work outside the home. The average parishioner age is mid-forties, with the majority holding college degrees. Father Art Baranowski began the concept of a restructured parish here. When he left, thirty-six small church communities existed.

Archdiocese of Dubuque, Iowa

St. Cecilia Church, Ames. St. Cecilia, with nearly 1,150 households, is staffed by three Conventual Franciscan Friars. More than half of the forty-seven thousand residents of Ames are Iowa State University students. In addition to the university, numerous federal and state agencies influence the community. Merging the scientific and religious dimensions of everyday life is an issue the community faces daily. The people of Ames and St. Cecilia's are financially well off, and the materialism of our society presents a constant tension with gospel living.

Diocese of Erie, Pennsylvania

St. Mark Catholic Center, Erie. Except for a few mid-sized cities, much of the diocese is rural. Mainly a middle- to lower-class area, the diocese includes the two poorest counties in the state. Two challenges that face the people of this diocese are unemployment and an increasing elderly population. Business and industry previously found in small towns have had to close, forcing young people to seek employment in larger metropolitan areas. These questions were prepared by a small community of diocesan employees who meet regularly to pray and share with one another.

Diocese of Evansville, Indiana

The Diocese of Evansville is primarily a rural diocese. Many of the original settlers and farmers were hardworking, industrious German immigrants.

St. Anthony Parish, Evansville. St. Anthony is located in Evansville (pop. 130,000), a town in the southern part of the diocese bordering Kentucky. Parishioners are deeply rooted in the area. The small parish is no longer the center of life for young Catholic families, where both parents work outside the home and children are involved in many non-parish activities.

Diocese of Fargo, North Dakota

The Diocese of Fargo is a small rural diocese with many farm families of German and Irish descent. The diocese has many small parishes with deeply rooted people. The cities of Fargo and Grand Forks have larger parishes. The changes in modern America have had a great impact in this diocese—busy society, death of the small family farm and the rise of large corporate farm business, both parents working outside the home and the loss of family time together. Ten parishes participated in the workshop.

Diocese of Fort Wayne-South Bend, Indiana

This small rural diocese has stable, hardworking people. In the two cities, Fort Wayne and South Bend, the old ethnic parishes are largely gone. The population is mostly Anglo with a few Hispanics. Many people are strongly interested in ongoing parish-based small communities but find it difficult to get parishes to make small church communities the focus of their pastoral direction.

St. Monica Parish, Mishawaka. St. Monica, founded in 1915, is a neighborhood parish of 1,050 families. Originally of Italian and German heritage, this community is now an eclectic blend of all nationalities, including a Vietnamese family that the parish helped bring to this country. The parish is composed of middle- to upper-class people. Small communities are an important direction for this parish.

St. John the Evangelist Church, Goshen. St. John the Evangelist parish includes approximately five hundred families in a population area of about thirty thousand and is the only Roman Catholic church in this predominately Mennonite community.

Diocese of Fort Worth, Texas

St. Michael Catholic Community, Bedford. Fort Worth is a diocese of small towns with an ever-growing number of first-generation Mexicans. St. Michael is a bedroom community of several thousand families, mostly from the north, transient and very busy.

Diocese of Gallup, Texas

Our Lady of Fatima Parish, Chinle, Arizona. The see city of the Diocese of Gallup is in New Mexico. The diocese includes the western part of New Mexico (Apache, Navajo and those parts of the Navajo and Hopi Reservations) and the eastern section of Arizona. The group that submitted questions is part of a lay ministry training group at Our Lady of Fatima Parish in Chinle (pop. 2,800). The people involved in the group are Navajo Native Americans. The Navajo People are the largest Indian tribe in the country; their reservation stretches into New Mexico, Arizona and Utah. The people of Chinle have just finished a hogan-shaped church that incorporates many Navajo views and beliefs. (A hogan is a six- or eight-sided ceremonial hut with an earth floor. Its shape symbolizes prayer and is the center of life for Navajos.)

Diocese of Grand Island, Nebraska

The Diocese of Grand Island, in the west-northwestern part of Nebraska, consists of large cattle ranches and small towns. Some priests oversee as many as three to four small-town parishes within their vicinity. Each small town (pop. approx. 100 to 200) has its own Catholic church. Twenty parishes attended the diocesan workshop.

Diocese of Great Falls, Montana

This diocese covers two-thirds of one of the largest states in the United States. Most towns are small, and parishes often are spread out. People are friendly and open and willing to travel for the sake of belonging to a small church community. Mining and related industries are on the decline and so are jobs. The state population is steadily declining. A number of parishes have begun to center on small church communities as the best way to bring people together.

Diocese of Green Bay, Wisconsin

The Diocese of Green Bay is a large rural diocese of mostly small towns located in the eastern part of the state. Over a third of the diocesan population is Catholic. The people are deeply rooted and move only when absolutely necessary. People are friendly, content with the simple things and open to change in Church life. Several parishes are restructuring into small church communities.

St. Mary of the Angels Parish, Green Bay. St. Mary is a small rural parish of three hundred families. It was originally established in 1899 as Our Lady of Czestochowa for people of Polish descent in Green Bay. In 1900 the Franciscans renamed the parish Our Lady of the Angels. People farm or work in the mills of nearby Appleton. The parish has a stable population; many families have lived here for generations.

Diocese of Harrisburg, Pennsylvania

The Diocese of Harrisburg, composed primarily of small towns and rural areas, is in a section of Pennsylvania that is nine percent Catholic.

St. Joseph Parish, York. St. Joseph Parish has two hundred families and is an urban community surrounded by farmland. York goes back to the days before the American Revolution and has several Catholic parishes, largely middle-class and white. It has a poor inner city and parishes do a lot of outreach. People who live here mainly commute to work in Philadelphia. Many problems found in other areas are on the rise here, such as drugs, homelessness, teen pregnancies, child abuse and unemployment. The Capuchin Fathers who staff this parish are committed to small church communities as their main direction.

Archdiocese of Hartford, Connecticut

Fifty percent of the population of the Hartford archdiocese is Catholic. Connecticut, one of the wealthiest states, still has large pockets of poverty. Cuts in military installations and production of military-related items are hurting employment. The city of Hartford has a large Puerto Rican population. Ten percent of the parishes of the archdiocese are working to make small church communities their primary focus. The archdiocese, which has an office for small church communities, envisions a new kind of Church and offers practical help to parishes.

Diocese of Helena, Montana

The Diocese of Helena covers the western forty percent of the huge state of Montana. Most parishes are small, and some are isolated. A number of parishes have missions a good distance from the parish center. People are less busy than those in large populated centers, friendly and willing to try small Christian communities.

St. Richard Parish, Columbia Falls. St. Richard is located in Columbia Falls at the western gateway to Glacier National Park. The rural parish is geographically vast (over thirty-five hundred square miles). Its members are employed in a variety of industrial, recreational and professional occupations. In two years ten small church communities have been formed; the parish is firmly committed to this direction.

Diocese of Honolulu, Hawaii

The diocese includes all of the Hawaiian Islands, as well as the Equatorial Islands: Palmyra, Washington, Fanning and Christmas. Catholics make up about twenty percent of the island population.

St. John Church, Honolulu. St. John Church is an inner-city parish in a densely populated, low-income, working-class area near the International Airport. Its fifteen hundred Catholic families represent a racial mix of eighty-five percent Filipino, five percent Samoan, and the rest, second and later generations of Portuguese, Puerto Rican, Hawaiian, Chinese and Japanese.

Sacred Heart Church, Honolulu. Sacred Heart Church, seventy-six years old and staffed by Maryknoll Fathers, is fifteen minutes from downtown Honolulu. It consists of twelve hundred families—racially mixed, multi-ethnic and multi-generational in a transient neighborhood. The small church concept is in its infancy.

Archdiocese of Indianapolis, Indiana

The Archdiocese of Indianapolis is a mixture of urban, suburban and rural areas. Catholics represent ten percent of the population. Diverse efforts at parish renewal have characterized the archdiocese. Recently, the focus has been on developing small discussion groups.

Office of Catholic Education. The group that developed the questions is comprised of four family units who have been together for about four years.

St. Joan of Arc, Indianapolis. St. Joan of Arc Parish in the past twenty years has evolved from a middle-class white community into a racially, culturally and economically diverse community of four hundred families in an area that is minimally Catholic.

Diocese of Joliet, Illinois

The Diocese of Joliet, located southwest of Chicago, is a growing diocese with many people moving here from nearby Chicago. More and more rural areas are being developed for residential and commercial use. The people are suburbanites: busy and largely middle class. Small communities are an important part of eighteen parishes and the main focus of a few.

Diocese of Kalamazoo, Michigan

St. Joseph Parish, Kalamazoo. In the Diocese of Kalamazoo Catholics represent only ten percent of the total population. Most parishes are in small towns and rural communities. St. Joseph is a fairly steady group of people (eleven hundred households with ten percent turnover per year). The parish, characterized by a generous spirit of service, warm hospitality and deep faith, struggles with questions of responsibility to the poor, how best to serve those who are grieving and how to respond to folks who are afflicted by or threatened with unemployment.

St. John the Evangelist Church, Benton Harbor. St. John is one hundred years old with three hundred fifty parishioners. Located in the "fruit belt" along the southeastern shore of Lake Michigan, it currently has five small church communities. They began as a spinoff of RENEW ten years ago.

Diocese of Kansas City-St. Joseph, Missouri

The metropolitan area of Kansas City is divided by the Missouri-Kansas state line as well as the Archdiocese of Kansas and the Diocese of Kansas City-St. Joseph. The Missouri side has a declining industrial base and an expanding poor community, while the Kansas side flourishes with the economic base of new technology and is surrounded by upper-income housing. The metropolitan area is fifteen percent Catholic; the rural area is nine percent Catholic. The diocese has been fortunate to have a history of progressive episcopal leadership. Twelve parishes from the diocese attended the small church community workshop.

St. Charles Borromeo Parish, Kansas City, Missouri. St. Charles is a suburban parish with approximately two thousand families, mostly middle- to lower middle-class income levels. St. Charles has a high degree of lay involvement in the parish, with multiple ministries coordinated by a large staff.

Guardian Angels Parish, Kansas City, Missouri. Guardian Angels parish is an older urban parish of approximately seven hundred families with a large number of elderly, singles and Hispanics. Guardian Angels at the present time is led by a pastoral administrator and assisted by a Jesuit priest.

Diocese of La Crosse, Wisconsin

The Diocese of La Crosse is mostly Caucasian with some Hmong, Native Americans and Vietnamese. The larger cities in the diocese are more heavily Catholic. The diocese is mostly rural with few mid-size cities. A small number of parishes attended the workshop on restructuring into small church communities. A few parishes are making small church communities the focus of their pastoral plan. Others pursue small communities as a program.

St. Olaf Parish, Eau Claire. St. Olaf is a relatively young parish, recently celebrating its fortieth anniversary. The parish is located on the north side of the city and is composed of about nine hundred thirty families: white, middle class and fairly young. This section of the city is growing and gaining a better image. The city of Eau Claire (pop. 55,000) is mostly white, lower- to upper-middle-class families. The area, once industrial, has become a retail and service area, with a large medical community affiliated with the Mayo Clinic and two hospitals. The largest manufacturer in the area closed last year, putting eleven hundred people out of work. Most have remained in the area looking for other work or retraining.

Diocese of Las Cruces, New Mexico

Immaculate Heart of Mary Cathedral, Las Cruces. The diocese is largely rural-agricultural. The industry is heavily government-related with White Sands and NASA located nearby. The cathedral, founded in 1954, has 2,925 families, mostly Anglo white (fifty-nine percent) and Hispanics. There is a mixture of young families with children and senior citizens. The questions were prepared by three different communities from the cathedral: "I Call You Friends," "Living Water" and "Purple Tigus."

Diocese of Lafayette, Louisiana

The Diocese of Lafayette, eight counties in the south central part of the state, is commonly referred to as "Cajun Country." The people are mostly descendants of French Canadians transported in the eighteenth century by the British from Nova Scotia. Many blacks have been Catholic for hundreds of years. The area is rural; farming is primarily sugar cane and cotton. The diocese is referred to as a home mission diocese since it is comprised entirely of missions and small-town parishes. Small communities are beginning in a number of parishes.

St. Anthony of Padua Parish, Eunice. St. Anthony is a parish of about two thousand families in a rural area, predominately white with a mixture of African-Americans and a few Vietnamese. The people are in middle- to lower-income levels and depend primarily on agriculture for work. The questions were developed by a small group of three women who have been meeting together for some time: ages fifty to fifty-eight, married and widowed, high school and college graduates.

Diocese of Lansing-Saginaw-Kalamazoo, Michigan

Pastors and leaders from the Dioceses of Lansing, Saginaw and Kalamazoo attended a small church communities workshop held in Lansing. All three dioceses are located in the southern part of Michigan. People are facing stessful times because of high unemployment, especially due to cutbacks in the automotive industry.

Archdiocese of Los Angeles, California

The archdiocese includes the counties of Los Angeles, Santa Barbara and Ventura. The Catholic population represents twenty-five percent of the total diocesan population. The metropolitan area is highly multi-ethnic and multi-racial, including large numbers of immigrants from many Asian countries. Catholic Asians are most often Filipinos and Vietnamese. Parishes usually have schools and have many different programs of all types. Both the southern California culture and parish life tend to be "on the go," making reflection difficult. A few parishes—Hispanic, Anglo and other mixed races—are slowly structuring into small church communities.

Santa Barbara is a two-hour drive north of Los Angeles. It has controlled growth by restricting new housing. Santa Barbara itself is well-to-do and living there is expensive. The county has a mix of people in mostly smaller towns. Several parishes, including a university parish, are gathering into small church communities.

Our Lady of the Assumption Church, Ventura. Our Lady of the Assumption is an older community in a beach town. A number of younger families have moved elsewhere for jobs. Some beach people look occasionally at the parish. Several small communities exist.

Archdiocese of Louisville, Kentucky

St. Bernard Catholic Church, Louisville. St. Bernard is thirty years old with twelve hundred families. They have an active ecumenical outreach with other churches in the area, as well as an outreach to Appalachia and Haiti. Their small communities consist of a good cross section of the parish: young, middle-aged, widowed and seniors.

Diocese of Madison, Wisconsin

The diocese is both urban and rural, in the south central part of the state. Catholic education and ministry to the handicapped are priorities of the people of this diocese.

St. Bernard Parish, Middleton. St. Bernard is an urban parish of almost five thousand parishioners. It continues to build small church communities through sharing the Sunday Gospel—in neighborhoods, with commissions, various interest groups and staff. The communities blend varied life-styles; people began by going through RENEW together, followed by Phase II on Prayer. Sharing the Sunday Gospel, outreach ministry and faith are important to the small church communities.

Diocese of Manchester, New Hampshire

Nashua Christian Life Center, Hudson. The Diocese of Manchester serves people from many ethnic backgrounds: French, Irish, Polish, Spanish. Professions range from farmer to blue-collar worker to professional. North of Manchester one finds rural settings and tourist sites. The greatest problem people face today is unemployment. Many families are caught up in an endless search for jobs and new directions. The group that gathered to create the life focus questions are connected to the Nashua Deanery Christian Life Center. They all belong to a parish and range from age twenty-eight to sixty. All meetings begin with reflective faith-sharing questions. The process has helped them to grow in their faith.

Diocese of Metuchen, New Jersey

The Diocese of Metuchen is chiefly suburban and semirural, although there are a few small cities such as New Brunswick, the site of Rutgers, the state university. The ethnic makeup of the diocese is Euro-American, Latino, African-American, Vietnamese, Korean, Filipino, Portuguese and Chinese. People struggle with the stress of unemployment, single-parent families and substance abuse. Seven parishes from the diocese and one from the nearby diocese of Allentown, Pennsylvania, participated in an in-depth workshop held in October, 1991. Three parishes have begun restructuring and the rest will do so upon completion of their RENEW programs.

Diocese of Monterey, California

The Diocese of Monterey has a population that is forty percent Hispanic and twenty percent Filipino, with pockets of Vietnamese and Korean on Monterey Island, and a small number of African-Americans. The remainder are of European origin, especially Yugoslavian, Portuguese and Italian. Ranching, fishing, business and blue-collar industries are some occupations in the diocese. Life is predominately rural, with small towns along the major highways. Many Mexicans work in the agriculture fields; Spanish is the predominate language. Salinas Valley is known as the salad bowl of the world. Life is filled with hardship for farmworkers who struggle to support their families. The children of these families straddle two societies and feel alien to both. The wealthy, the middle class and the poor can meet on common ground in the parish. Pastors are constantly challenged to bring the groups together in common liturgies. Seven parishes participated in a workshop on small church communities.

Diocese of Nashville, Tennessee

Catholic Center, Nashville. In an area sometimes called the "Buckle of the Bible Belt," Catholics in this middle Tennessee diocese must live their faith under real pressure as religious minorities, since they are surrounded by a variety of Protestant and fundamentalist churches who constantly evangelize Catholics. Several parishes are committed to structuring into small church communities as the main focus of the parish. The questions were formulated by the Ministry Formation Services team. The team consists of eight women—single parents, married, single and religious. Ages range from early thirties to mid-sixties.

Archdiocese of Newark, New Jersey

Annunciation Parish, Paramus. Newark is in decline, with high unemployment and crime. It has strong ethnic neighborhoods, primarily Portuguese and Italian, as well as large black and Puerto Rican populations. Annunciation Parish, in Paramus, is northwest of Newark with beautiful countryside and middle- to upper-class parishioners. The poor and rich, geographically segregated, don't have the chance to mix well.

Archdiocese of New Orleans, Louisiana

The Archdiocese of New Orleans, celebrating its bicentennial in 1993, is over one-third Catholic. Ten parishes participated in a workshop on structuring into small church communities.

Resurrection of Our Lord Parish, New Orleans. Resurrection of Our Lord Parish, located in the eastern suburbs of New Orleans, serves sixteen hundred families and is a pioneer parish in furthering small church communities within the parish and throughout the archdiocese. The parish is multicultural, including whites, African-Americans and Asians. The parishioners are middle class, blue collar and professional with high school and college educations. They have begun a parish and school development process aimed at creating a spiritually active, morally strong and financially sound environment within a multicultural community in which all members are church for each other.

St. Peter Parish, Covington. St. Peter is committed to restructuring into small church communities. Thirty-five to forty parish leaders and the pastor attended a three-day retreat to plan the process of restructuring. The parish has adapted the vision and small church communities have developed.

Archdiocese of New York, New York

The Archdiocese of New York has a great variety of immigrants from all over the world. Great numbers of Spanish-speaking Hispanics from Puerto Rico, Cuba and Central America have moved into the city, as have French-speaking Haitians. The city has both highly educated people with great wealth and influence and the very poor and homeless. The Church includes all of these. The archdiocese also includes many small towns and suburbs located north of the city. People are quite busy, have long commutes to work and tend to keep their convictions and values to themselves. Small communities can bring people together, and a few parishes in very different parts of the archdiocese are moving in this direction.

Church of St. Francis Xavier, New York City. St. Francis Xavier is an urban church with a very mobile group of parishioners, mostly middle class in the lower end of Manhattan. St. Francis Xavier is not a "geographic" parish but rather an intentional community with many parishioners traveling a great distance to attend parish functions. People are motivated and willing to connect their everyday life with their faith.

Diocese of Norwich, Connecticut

Thirteen parishes from the Norwich diocese attended the workshop on small church communities. One is a Spanish-speaking community, mostly poor Puerto Ricans. The diocese has much open agricultural land. Some people are farmers, but many people work in light industry or professions in the larger cities. This is a middle-class area in a recession, and families are experiencing a lot of social pressures.

Archdiocese of Oklahoma City, Oklahoma

St. John the Baptist Church, Edmond. St. John the Baptist is a parish of twenty-six hundred families located in a northern suburb of Oklahoma City. The parish is struggling for a sense of community because it is so large and the people are highly mobile.

Archdiocese of Omaha, Nebraska

The Archdiocese of Omaha is basically a rural area; Omaha is its largest city and has the greatest percentage of the population. Nebraska has a low unemployment rate (three percent) compared to other states. The diocese boasts many Catholic schools in average-income communities.

St. Stanislaus Parish, Omaha. St. Stanislaus is a small parish in the Polish community of South Omaha. It has a large percentage of elderly and retired members. It does, however, house and support a grade school in cooperation with two other neighboring parishes. The core group at St. Stanislaus consists of nine people: the pastor, the religious staff and five parishioners who had been involved in RENEW and continued to meet in small faith-sharing groups afterward. Their goal is to establish small church groups within the parish.

Diocese of Orange, California

Roughly fifty percent of the Church in Orange County is Hispanic and about ten percent is Asian; both ethnic groups have been increasing steadily while the Anglo population has remained about the same. Economically, Church membership spans a wide spectrum. People face a fast pace of life, complicated by a high rate of mobility and a consumeristic mentality that can significantly limit time for attentiveness to and reflection on the presence of God in their lives.

Diocese of Paterson, New Jersey

St. Nicholas Catholic Church, Passaic. St. Nicholas Church, one hundred twenty-five years old, is an inner-city, multicultural parish with lower- to middle-income families. Sunday and weekday liturgies are offered in English and Spanish, and major feasts are usually bilingual.

Diocese of Peoria, Illinois

St. Francis of Assisi Newman Center, Western Illinois University, Macomb. The students at the Newman Center at Western Illinois University have all been involved in the Challenge Program of Mark Link in small groups. This is their first taste of small church communities.

Archdiocese of Philadelphia, Pennsylvania

St. Andrew Parish, Newtown. St. Andrew Parish, founded in 1880, is located in a northern rural-suburban area about forty-five minutes from the center of Philadelphia. It is a rapidly growing parish; during the last twelve years it has grown from eight hundred to over thirty-one hundred families. The parish is a bedroom community for the cities of Philadelphia, New Jersey and New York. The average income is in the middle to upper brackets and the average age is thirty-three. The people here need a more personal and belonging community, a community that cares and shares faith experiences and provides support in dealing with life's problems. The small community that submitted the questions consists of six couples and a Marianist brother.

St. William Parish, Philadelphia. St. William is located in a white, middle-class, conservative, Catholic neighborhood. St. William and other parishes in the archdiocese are presently pursuing the plan for making small church communities the focus direction of their parishes.

Diocese of Phoenix, Arizona

The Phoenix area has grown steadily since World War II. There is a mix of rich and poor, old and young, Anglos and Mexican-Americans, as well as newly arrived Mexicans. Some parishes are extremely well off and some are very poor, with little interaction between them. Several parishes are committed to the effort to restructure the parish into small church communities.

Diocese of Pittsburgh, Pennsylvania

St. Margaret Church, Pittsburgh. The diocese consists of one large metropolitan area surrounded by small towns and rural areas. Because of a considerable decline in Catholic population in the last twenty years, the diocese has been through a long process of merging parishes. St. Margaret Church is experiencing this same loss. Immigrants who worked the mines and steel mills, which are mostly gone today, once filled the old ethnic European parishes. The new work is high tech. Younger and more educated people are relocating to the suburbs outside the diocesan area.

Diocese of Providence, Rhode Island

The Diocese of Providence has the second largest number of senior citizens in the country and the largest percent of Catholics per capita in the United States. The Church is easily taken for granted, and young people are formed more by culture than by Church. The Northeast has suffered from declining industry and job loss for many years. A significant number of parishes are pursuing small church communities as the parish focus to help make faith an everyday part of life. Those who formulated these questions were from five urban, suburban and rural parishes ranging in size from five hundred fifty to three thousand families of mostly Portuguese, Italian, Irish and French descent.

St. Jude Parish, Lincoln. St. Jude, a community of seventeen hundred families in a suburb of Providence, currently has four vibrant small church communities that have been meeting for about a year. The diocese has a number of parishes centering on small church communities, and these parishes meet in a local alliance. Some of these parishes will become models of this new kind of parish.

St. Lucy Parish, Middletown. St. Lucy is a parish of sixteen hundred families with diverse economic profiles. Reflecting the diversity present in the larger community, the parish includes farmers, tradespeople, teachers and professors, transitional and retired military, and numerous specialty professions, particularly those employed within the military-industrial complex. These families reflect a mixed ethnic background, particularly Portuguese and Filipino. Most, though not all of these groups, are reflected within the small church communities.

Diocese of Raleigh, North Carolina

In the Diocese of Raleigh Catholics are a small minority (about ten percent) and are still seen as different. They are a committed minority, however. Parishes are small but growing. In cities such as Raleigh, Durham and Chapel Hill, people can easily belong to a parish without knowing or affecting other parishioners. People can spend their time making a living without making a connection between their work and faith lives. Several parishes are structuring into small church communities as a way of countering this tendency.

Diocese of Reno-Las Vegas, Nevada

St. Andrew Church, Boulder City. St. Andrew is a community of six hundred families. Many of the residents of Boulder City are of retirement age, settled in their various traditions, including that of Church, which makes growing in the spirit of Vatican II a challenge, and one that is painful for some.

Diocese of Richmond, Virginia

Parish of the Holy Spirit, Virginia Beach. The small community that composed these questions consists of fifteen members, a mixed group: married, divorced, single, male and female, various ages. They have been together for four years. Holy Spirit Parish is committed to restructuring into small church communities.

Diocese of Rockford, Illinois

Fifty-five percent of the Catholic population of the diocese lives in the western suburbs of Chicago; they are traditional, professional, white, upper-class people. Those living in the city of Rockford are lower middle-class people working in industrial plants. The balance of the diocese is rural-agricultural, with many small towns of older people who are less educated with lower incomes.

Sts. Peter and Paul Church, Cary. Sts. Peter and Paul Parish, eighty-one years old, is located in the northeast end of Rockford. The people are of a mixed culture and range from very young to middle age. The parish was at one time considered rural; presently people find work in light industry or with the Northwestern Railroad, or commute to downtown Chicago. Small church communities have been in existence for four years.

Diocese of Rockville Centre, New York

Because of its position at the eastern end of Long Island, many people in the Rockville Centre diocese have a long and wearisome commute to work each day in New York City. People experience the pressures of a shrinking middle class. The diocese has experienced several waves of new immigrants—Puerto Ricans and Filipinos, as well as others who tend to be less Catholic as a nationality.

The Church of the Good Shepherd, Holbrook. Good Shepherd Parish is not yet twenty years old. Currently, it has over four thousand registered families who live in an area of about nine square miles. Holbrook is located on Long Island, about fifty miles out from Manhattan. Many adults commute to the city to work, but a significant number work on Long Island as teachers, nurses, police officers and firefighters. The civic community of Holbrook is suburban and ranges economically from middle-class to lower middle-income. With an average age of forty-one, this is definitely a baby boomer community with lots of children. The parish doesn't have a parochial school, so religious education takes place in homes; over twenty-four hundred youngsters attend. The parish is three years into the process of restructuring into small church communities. Though only one hundred sixty people are actively involved in the process, all parish meetings, programs and activities use the small group reflections on life experience, prayer and faith-sharing dynamic of the small church communities.

Diocese of St. Augustine, Florida

St. Augustine boasts the oldest Catholic settlement in the United States, dating back to the Spanish settlers in the early 1800's. The diocese includes a large military installation in Jacksonville, a multi-ethnic metro area (largely Hispanic) and a state university. Although the Catholic population is small, its presence spans several generations. small church communities are growing thoughout the diocese. A few leadership people are beginning to see small church communities as the pastoral plan of their parishes.

Archdiocese of St. Louis, Missouri

St. Louis has a strong faith history. Its Catholic academic institutions include three universities and colleges, twenty-nine high schools and 177 elementary schools. The archdiocese also has many social and missionary programs. In 1956 priests were sent to Bolivia to begin a Latin America Apostolate that is still supported and staffed by the archdiocese. The first Catholic school west of the Mississippi was founded in St. Louis by St. Rose Philippine Duchesne. Ten percent of St. Louis parishes have attended the first workshop on small church communities. Three local alliances exist today.

Sts. John and James Parish, Ferguson. Sts. John and James Parish is a large, active, well-established parish with a grade school. Parishioners are predominantly white, middle- to upper-class and of all ages. The parish is always one of the first to accept and complete forward moving programs from the archdiocese. This is one of the most promising models of restructuring into small church communities.

Archdiocese of St. Paul-Minneapolis, Minnesota

Most people of the archdiocese are white, middle- to upper-class, from both urban and rural areas. Relationships tend to be close, and people reach out to one another. The major non-white ethnic population is Hmong, followed by Hispanic and African-American. Many Native American people live throughout the state. While most parishes still have resident priest-pastors, parish communities are using different processes to plan for the time when this will not be true. On Sundays, time is provided around the Sunday assembly for programs and community building.

Archdiocese of San Antonio, Texas

San Antonio covers the southern counties of the state near the Mexican border. Most of the people are Mexican-Americans. San Antonio itself is sixty percent Hispanic. Outside of San Antonio, the rest of the archdiocese is composed of small towns and rural areas. People find work in farming and on or near the many military bases in the area. Great community organizing has been done here; poor and uneducated people can move the local government to respond to social needs. Parishes are very interested in structuring into small church communities. The questions came from eleven parishes that participated in the workshop and are planning to focus their parishes into small church communities.

St. Anthony of Padua Parish, San Antonio. The questions were formulated by a small community in the parish (eight women and one man) that has been together since the beginning of RENEW. They hope to continue as a small community after RENEW.

St. Francis of Assisi Catholic Community, Laughlin Air Force Base. This is the largest Air Force Base in the world and has the largest chapel. The median age of the parish is late twenties. Some military personnel are quite transient (boot camp is six months), but retired military personnel and dependents are more permanent residents here. Foreign military students are an important, although temporary, part of the parish. One small community of nine men and women contributed these questions.

Diocese of San Bernardino, California

The Diocese of San Bernardino includes the huge Mojave Desert. Most parishes have one Mass in Spanish; a few parishes have more Spanish Masses than English. The vicar and associate bishop are Hispanic. All but the smaller parishes have about fifteen hundred families per priest.

Diocese of San Diego, California

Our Lady of Perpetual Help Church, Lakeside. Our Lady of Perpetual Help is a parish of approximately two thousand families in a rural suburb of San Diego. The parish has a small-town atmosphere, and most parishioners have lived in the area for many years. They are mostly working-class, non-professionals. Their strong sense of community and family has been enhanced by the small church communities. The parish is committed to restructuring into small church communities, and they are the main focus of parish life. This commitment began in 1990 and today there are twenty active small communities. Some type of faith sharing is part of all parish activities, and people are becoming closer to one another and to God through sharing life and faith experiences. The questions used for this book were developed by two small church communities during their regular meeting time.

Archdiocese of San Francisco, California

San Francisco's population includes both the very rich and the very poor. It has an ever-growing number of Spanish-speaking Mexican-Americans, as well as a sizeable gay community. Several parishes attended the workshop on restructuring parishes into small church communities.

Most Holy Redeemer Parish, San Francisco. Holy Redeemer is in the Mission District, the gay section of San Francisco. The parish is "eighty percent gay and twenty percent gray"; the senior and homosexual populations mix well. The parish's outreach to people dying of AIDS is known throughout the city; the hospitality and welcome shown to gay people is a tribute to Most Holy Redeemer. Many professionals from all over the United States live here.

Diocese of San Jose, California

St. Maria Goretti Parish, San Jose. The Diocese of San Jose is a very young diocese, having been established in 1981. The diocese has mixed ethnic groups, predominantly Hispanic with some Filipino and Vietnamese. Present parish structures are challenged by the rapid growth of the Catholic population. Anglo parishioners at St. Maria Goretti Parish have become a minority. First-generation Mexican-Americans, the largest group in the parish, are often very poor. They work long and hard and struggle to make ends meet. The rest of the parish population is Asian—Vietnamese and Filipino. The parish is committed to small church communities in Spanish and English. The "Mustard Seed Community" consists entirely of Filipinos and has been meeting for two and a half years.

Archdiocese of Santa Fe, New Mexico

The Catholic Church has been deeply involved in the history of New Mexico. The spirituality of the archdiocese is reflected in great part in the cultural and religious traditions of the Hispanic and Native American peoples.

Archdiocese of Seattle, Washington

St. Anthony Parish, Renton. Instead of closing churches because of the priest shortage, the Archdiocese of Seattle has a plan called "Viable Faith Community," in which parishes have a lay pastor or a cluster of parishes shares resources. Small faith communities fit into this plan as a means of maintaining life and hope among its people. St. Anthony is a parish of about twenty-five hundred families with two priests. The people are primarily middle class, multi-ethnic and multicultural. The size of the parish makes personal connection among the parishioners difficult. Small faith-sharing groups offer a way for people to get connected. The groups are still loosely structured, but a core team meets weekly to make sure these groups are connected to the parish and to discuss and work on ways to grow and spread the good news of small faith-sharing groups. The group that developed the questions consists of singles, divorced and married, young and middle-aged parish members.

Diocese of Spokane, Washington

St. Mary Parish, Spokane. St. Mary is a middle-class parish with many activities. It has been committed for several years to restructuring into small church communities. The Northwest is the most unchurched part of the United States, and small church communities are the means by which many parishes try to encourage people to connect everyday life and faith.

Diocese of Springfield, Illinois

The Diocese of Springfield is largely rural. The major population centers are Decatur, Springfield, the Metro East area of St. Louis, Quincy and Effingham.

Diocese of Steubenville, Ohio

Parishes in the Diocese of Steubenville tend to be small and distant from each other. Because most of the steel mills have closed, causing high unemployment, many young people are leaving the area. Bishop Ottenweller, retired in 1992, has encouraged the priests in the diocese to move their parishes toward small church communities.

Diocese of Toledo, Ohio

The Diocese of Toledo is a largely rural diocese with many small towns scattered throughout. Industry in the Toledo area has declined, and people face serious unemployment. Toledo has a large black population and some second- and third-generation Mexican-Americans. The diocese faces the difficult decision of closing or combining city parishes.

Diocese of Tucson, Arizona

The Diocese of Tucson covers southern Arizona from California to New Mexico. The diocese is tri-cultural: Anglo, Hispanic and Native American. Tucson (pop. 700,000) is the only urban area. About twenty-five percent of Tucson is Hispanic. The other towns, centered on mining or agriculture, are mainly Hispanic. Native Americans live mostly on reservations. Although southern Arizona is becoming a popular retirement area, the median age of metro Tucson is about thirty-three. Unemployment is low, but too many people are employed in low- to minimum-wage jobs.

Diocese of Tulsa, Oklahoma

The rural areas of the Diocese of Tulsa have mostly poor farming parishes. Urban Tulsa is industrial with a middle-class population. The diocese has a small percentage of Native Americans, blacks and Hispanics.

St. James Parish, Bartlesville. St. James parishioners are in the upper-middle-class income bracket. Most work at an affluent white-collar company, where downsizing is causing stress and uncertainty. The parish has been moving toward the structure of small church communities for several years.

Diocese of Venice, Florida

The small church community that submitted the questions includes teachers, homemakers and retirees. It has a mix of black and white members. Many members live in a federal housing project.

Archdiocese of Washington, Washington, D.C.

Much of the city is poor, with many minority neighborhoods, high crime and unemployment. Other parts of the city, home to those involved with the government, are quite wealthy. These two groups do not mix well. A few parishes are attempting small church communities, but most are not yet ready. These questions come from six parishes at a workshop for restructuring the parish.

Diocese of Wheeling-Charleston, West Virginia

Catholic Church of the Ascension, Hurricane. The Diocese of Wheeling-Charleston covers the entire state of West Virginia. At the Catholic Church of the Ascension, a small community of four women that meets weekly for Scripture sharing prepared these questions.

St. Theresa Parish, Morgantown. St. Theresa parish membership ranges from lower middle-class to affluent. Educational background ranges from eighth grade to college. Forty men and women are involved in five small church communities.

Diocese of Worcester, Massachusetts

Religious Education Office, Worcester. The Diocese of Worcester is predominantly rural, although it has a strong and diversified industrial base. Because an increase in technological industry has caused a shift in population to the suburbs, urban parishes find themselves with fewer parishioners. Nearly half the parishes in the diocese participated in RENEW, and many parishes have continued to support small faith groups.

St. Augustine Community, Worcester. This community includes four Assumptionist religious and four young candidates to the Assumptionist life. They are all involved in formation work, a publishing center called Assumption Communications and in teaching and campus ministry at Assumption College. They are using the materials published for small church communities for their own community meetings with good results.

Diocese of Yakima, Washington

The Diocese of Yakima is a predominantly rural community, with a high concentration of fruit growers. Fifty percent of the Catholic population is Hispanic; a small percentage is Oriental and black.

Diocese of Youngstown, Ohio

The city of Youngstown is declining as many steel mills shut down or cut back. High unemployment has led to a loss of both population and a sense of hope for the future. Canton has more optimism. The rest of the diocese consists of small towns and rural areas, with a more stable population.

Appendix B

Small Church Communities Outside the United States

Africa

Kenya

St. Peter Claver Church, Nairobi. St. Peter Claver is an old parish of the Holy Ghost Fathers on the edge of the industrial area. The city has built up around the parish so it is a drop-in place for many people: prisoners, tribesmen coming through the bus station nearby, priests and seminarians on holiday from other missions. The people of the parish are involved in a small core of activities. Many groups call themselves basic Christian communities, and they are aware of justice issues and have an open-door attitude to everything that occurs around them. They are middle class by African standards and are wonderfully caring and hospitable to everyone.

South Africa

Broken Wall Community, Cape Town. The Broken Wall Community was established to provide a place where both black and white people can live together and work out their repentance in relationship with one another. The established policy in South Africa has been effective in keeping people apart in language, living areas, education, social development and worship. This policy has created suspicion, anger, hatred, fear, oppression and economic greed among the different racial groups.

Chase Valley, Pietermaritzburg. This small church community consists of men and women, all retired (fifty to seventy years old) middle class, with average education, facing the challenge of living the gospel in a changing South Africa.

Sudan

Diocese of El Obeid

Christians in El Obeid are influenced by persecution of the Church by Muslim fundamentalists, civil war and ethnic division. The five Expatriate Fathers in El Nohud were told that their presence may soon be terminated by the Internal Security. This is a warning of sad things to come.

Tanzania

St. Jude Thaddeus Small Christian Community, Musoma. Christians are unable to practice their faith openly and the future is very bleak. They are determined to continue, however, and a Basic Ecclesial Community workshop was scheduled in the Mission Institute in 1993.

Zimbabwe

All Souls Catholic Mission, Binga. The questions were prepared by a small church community comprised of Batonga people of Zimbabwe in southern Africa. Known as the "river people," the Batonga formerly lived along the banks of the Zambezi River and were great hunters, fishermen and farmers. Now that they live in a remote area far from adequate water supply, the Batonga are subsistence farmers who daily face the threat of wild animals and drought. Amid severe hunger and poverty, the faith of the Batonga people has given birth to new Christian communities.

Asia

Japan

St. Augustine Kasai Catholic Church, Tokyo. Questions were formulated by a group consisting of ten Japanese women, all converts from the Buddist tradition. They all find that faith in Jesus has freed them from many culturally imposed stereotypes and from the superstition that paralyzes many good people around them.

New Guinea

Catechist Training Center Fissoa, Kavieng, New Ireland Proving, Papua. New Guinea, an independent Third World country, is the second largest island in the world. The land is very fertile and agriculture is the primary industry. Three million people speak approximately seven hundred different languages, although English is considered the official language. Much unrest exists, especially between tribes. Since the mid-1970's, people have moved from tribal traditions to embracing Western culture. Since the arrival of missionaries in the 1950's, New Guinea is considered a Christian country, with Catholics being the largest denomination. New Guinea Catholic liturgies include many tribal traditions. Many of their clergy, including bishops, are native-born. Small church communities on the South American model are called New Image of the Parish (NIPs). The bishops are strongly urging the parishes to adopt NIPs.

Philippines

Blessed Sacrament Congregation, Assumption Parish, Davao City. Davao City is in the Tagum area, a mountain range running the length of the island. The Cebuane language is the only language used in the Tagum area. Beginning in the 1960's, the fifty-eight thousand people in this area were reevangelized and structured into seventy-two ecclesial communities, each with approximately two hundred families. These communities are concerned with social issues such as health programs, efforts at land reform and just wages. The people live in barrios, are not well educated but have been coming into the center regularly for training since the early 1960's. Native priests and seminarians go out to each community once a month. Assumption Parish, in the port city of Davao City, is run by the Blessed Sacrament Fathers. They have an exceptionally well-educated clergy with ties to the United States and Canada. The people are middle class by Philippine standards—businesspeople, teachers, bankers, shopkeepers—and all interested in education for their children. They are nervous about the political action of the Tagum area. They started the groups on the model of the Tagum communities but have taken another orientation.

Taiwan, Republic of China

Fengshan City. There are three churches in this area: Blessed Sacrament, a workers' chapel and another parish. This is a port city with amenities such as gas, electricity and running water. The people are middle class by Chinese standards. They are under martial law now, but with a popular Taiwanese president. Communist China is a constant threat. People talk of uprisings from time to time, and they even speak of invading the mainland, but that always comes to nothing. The people are predominantly young and hardworking; few are without jobs. The older people stay in the villages, and only the young go to the port city for the most part.

Australia

Archdiocese of Melbourne, Victoria

Melbourne is an industrial and cultured metropolitan diocese with high unemployment. As in any similar Western environment, people tend to be busy, overextended and unreflective.

Diocese of Rockhampton, Queensland

Nineteen parishes attended the workshop. The parishes included coastal resort towns, mining towns with a transient population and outback parishes with scattered centers for Sunday liturgies and only a handful of Catholic families. A religious sister with a pilot's license flies to the most remote areas to gather people into small communities. One parish is in an Aborigines' settlement in the outback.

Callide Valley Parish, Biloela Q. Biloela is a mining and herding area. The parish includes hundreds of square miles with several smaller towns or communities within the parish. People in these rural areas are very open to meeting with each other and seek human companionship. The distances make meeting difficult. One rural community suggested phone conferencing.

Diocese of Townsville, Queensland

This is a huge territory with outback for livestock and some mining. Parishes often are hundreds of thousands of square kilometers, and people live far apart from each other. There is a real clergy shortage. But, people work hard and enjoy simple pleasures and look forward to social contacts. Because of the great distances between people, the use of teleconferencing (telephones) for the small church community has been suggested.

Diocese of Port Pirie, Whyalla Stuart

Whyalla West Parish, Our Lady Help of Christians Church, Whyalla Stuart. The town of Whyalla is located on Spencers Gulf in southern Australia. The people are caring, friendly and sincere, somewhat more laid back than the city dwellers. Large sheep stations surround the town, but steel is Whyalla's major industry. Unemployment is not a stranger to these people. Whyalla's orange-red soil gives evidence of its nearness to its outback, as does the flat, arid country where emus and kangaroos roam in the wild. Until about twenty-five years ago, St. Theresa was the only Catholic Church in Whyalla. Then Our Lady Help of Christians was established to serve the growing Catholic community.

Europe

England

Hope Community, Wolverhampton. Hope Community was set up on Heath Town Estate in Wolverhampton. For the first twelve months, the community consisted of three women of the Sisters of the Infant Jesus. This community was extended to men and women in various walks of life. The community is best described as a series of concentric circles: the Sisters of the Infant Jesus, others who have committed to living with them for various lengths of time, and neighbors and friends who are involved with them in many different ways.

Post Green Community, Dorset. This community was formally established as an ecumenical lay Christian community in 1974. The principal calling of the community is to provide a place of refuge where people can grow toward their full potential within a safe and loving family environment, no matter what their present condition in life. The work of the community stresses self-development and personal growth. People of other faiths or of none and of whatever race, color or social class are welcomed and respected.

Ireland

County Sligo. This is a small group of professional people brought together by Father Jarlath Cunnane, a board member of the National Alliance. Parishes in Ireland don't seem to be restructuring into small church communities at this time. But the Church is changing, and young people especially no longer have an automatic loyalty to the Church. The materialistic culture is beginning to form people more than the faith. Unemployment is quite high with no solution in sight. It is a good time to bring people together in small church communities.

Lithuania

Lithuania Exchange Students, Lithuania Summer Camp, Camp Neringa, Brattleboro, Vermont. After fifty years of total repression under the atheistic Soviet state, the Church is free to exist and be recognized. The consciousness of the people has been maimed. The faithful do not have adequate post-Vatican II training, which calls for great social, cultural and religious sensitivity. The students who worked on these questions said that because their faith was forbidden, they wanted to know why it was forbidden or why they were being denied access to it. Once you break the ice of the faith search, the search for faith continues and you begin to strive for it and grow in faith. The Spirit begins to work in you, and you are led to an ever-deepening understanding of God and God's life in you and your life in God. The Lithuanians have experienced so many quarrels, divisions and factions that they find that every attempt to understand their enemy better leads to tolerance, acceptance and sometimes even unity.

North America

Canada

Diocese of Calgary, Alberta

The Diocese of Calgary covers southern Alberta from the Rocky Mountain Range eastward through vast prairie and ranchlands to the province of Saskatchewan. It consists of eighty parishes.

Archdiocese of Edmonton, Alberta

Our Lady of Perpetual Help Parish, Sherwood Park. This large parish (over three thousand families) is an active parish, yet involvement in all ministries seems to have declined over the last few years. The parishioners are in need of fresh insights. They presently have three small church communities.

Diocese of Hamilton, Ontario

The Diocese of Hamilton has a good balance of urban, suburban, small town and rural parishes. A few of these parishes have four to five thousand families. The diocese is multicultural. Due to the depressed state of Canada's economy, the unemployment rate at present averages about twelve percent throughout the diocese.

Diocese of London

Office of RENEW, Ontario. The Diocese of London is an area of great cultural diversity; it is rich in beautiful farmland and also home to many manufacturing centers, the majority of which are automotive related. A number of committed parishes are restructuring into small church communities.

Essex County, Cottam. The people of Essex County are similar to those in Michigan, with the same industries, terrain, concerns and culture. As a result of the recession, people are cutting back and living more stringent lives. On the positive side, families are staying home more and seem to find social activities at home rather than looking elsewhere. Another noticeable change this year is that church attendance is up, and people are more willing to share their food and clothing with those less fortunate. The Good Shepherd prayer group, a community of a dozen women who meet on Monday evenings, has been together for about eight years.

Archdiocese of St. Boniface, Manitoba

Nine parishes within the diocese are pursuing small church communities as the pastoral plan of the parish. They use both English and French resources. This diocese is across the river from Winnipeg and was the original French diocese reaching to the Pacific. Today, many new English-speaking families from Winnipeg and elsewhere are moving into its parishes. Its main challenge is to help people see the connection between their faith and the events of their busy work and family lives.

Diocese of St. Paul, Alberta

St. John the Baptist Church, Fort McMurray. This diocese has a number of French-speaking communities. It stretches across Alberta just north of the Edmonton Archdiocese. Its eastern border extends north to the Northwest Territories. It has twenty parishes and fifty missions.

Archdiocese of Toronto, Ontario

This is the largest city and diocese in Canada. It is a large urban center of business and commerce. The original English and Irish settlers were gradually outnumbered by Italian and other European immigrants. The last wave of immigrants has included Asians, Latin Americans and people from the Middle East. The clergy represent many of these ethnic groups. The city and parishes have experienced a rapid ethnic shift. Several parishes are structuring into small church communities.

Epiphany of Our Lord, Scarboro. Epiphany of Our Lord parish has a forty percent Italian population. They have seven Italian small church communities and use an Italian translation of the SCC resources. Epiphany is one of the most promising parishes structuring into small church communities in the Toronto Archdiocese.

Archdiocese of Vancouver, British Columbia

St. Joseph the Worker Parish, Richmond. St. Joseph the Worker is a large parish with a school and is serviced by the Graymoor Fathers. The population is mostly white, middle-to upper-class, with a recent influx of Asians. The parish council, commissions and parish leaders attended a weekend workshop on restructuring, and the parish is working at implementing the principles of restructuring into small church communities.

Honduras

Guajiquiro, La Paz. Guajiquiro is composed of poor, native people whose ancestors come from the Lecan Indians. The people work mainly in agriculture, raising basic foods. They are somewhat isolated from other areas due to lack of dependable transportation. They lack modern conveniences such as electricity and running water, but they are a happy, family-centered people, conscious of the common good.

South America

Brazil

Nova Descoberta, Detroit-Recife. Staffed by Detroit archdiocesan priests and the Immaculate Heart of Mary Sisters, the parish includes one hundred thousand people. The Recife area has over one million people, most of whom are poor, always have been poor and usually expect to remain poor. Dom Helder Camara encouraged people to meet in small groups to apply the gospel to the social situation and to work together for change. Small communities continue to do this.

Chile

Nirivillo, Santiago. The cities are large like any American or European city, and the people are so mixed that they do not identify Indians or classes. The language is Spanish throughout all the churches. Politically it is in the third year of democracy after sixteen years of dictatorship, and many of the old laws are still in effect. The groups are oriented to prayer, Scripture and justice. Justice concerns are basic to their personal lives rather than political protest. Parish life includes fiestas, social affairs, charitable functions and care for the poor through clothing and food drives. Fundamentalist sects are active among the Catholics, who have learned much from them. Only the Mormons resist ecumenical relationships. Nirivillo is located in the hills of southern Chile.

Peru

Sao Paulo, Puno. Peru is a republic in west South America with a population of 21.3 million people. Its capital, Lima, is predominately Spanish. The people of this area suffer oppression and racial discrimination.